BUTTERFLIES

of Grand Teton & Yellowstone National Park

by Steven Poole

Grand Teton Association
PO Box 170
Moose, WY 83012
www.grandtetonpark.org

Project Manager: Jan Lynch, Executive Director, GTA
Photographer and illustrator (except as noted): Steven Poole
Designer: Carole Thickstun
Printing: Paragon Press, Salt Lake City, UT

ISBN 978-0-931895-71-5

Grand Teton Association is a nonprofit publisher of books and
other materials about Grand Teton National Park and the
surrounding public lands.

*Dedicated to Pat Matheny and Emily Poole, whose
enthusiastic conversation about insects provided the spark that
led me to produce this book.*

Table of Contents

FRITILLARYS, medium or large, orange to brown, patterned with black on upperside and usually with white or silver spots on underside.

LESSER FRITILLARYS, small or medium, orange to brown, patterned with black on upperside, white bands rather than spots on underside, variable patterns.

CRESCENTS, small to medium, brown or orange, marked black, yellow, white on upperside, light tan or orange with white and or black markings on underside.

CHECKERSPOTS, small to medium, generally black veins make colored bands checkered, various tones black, white, red, and or orange.

ANGLEWINGS, COMMAS & TORTOISESHELLS, medium, upperside orange or brown, marking black white, yellow, blue, underside earthen gray or browns.

ADMIRALS, large, black with white upperside, white, red, and black undersides.

LADYS & ROYALTY, medium to large, upperside orange or red patterned with black or white, underside; variable in Ladys, similar to upperside in Royalty.

RINGLETS & WOOD NYMPHS, medium, tan or brown, with eyespots.

ALPINES & SATYR, medium, brown or black usually with eyespots, and orange or yellow markings.

THE BUTTERFLY, FASCINATING AND BEAUTIFUL, has been admired by people throughout the ages. Its form is used in rituals, art, and text, to symbolize beauty, freedom, love, and rebirth. Humans will also scorn the butterfly for the destruction that the larval stage can cause, eating the foliage from trees and devastating entire fields of crops.

Whether we notice them or not the butterflies contribute more than sheer beauty to our ecosystem. The butterfly is an indicator species that can tell us much about the current state of our environment. They can display changes from hour to hour, day to day, and year to year. Is the sun shining and the temperature warm? Has it been raining or frosty? Is the season's weather cool and damp, or warm and dry? These changes can affect the butterfly in many ways—when they fly, when they hatch, or what they eat.

Butterflies are especially vulnerable to pressures from our human population. Widespread use of pesticides and herbicides and the spread of invasive plant species are threats to the butterfly population. Even the "natural insecticide" Bt (*Bacillus thuringiensis*) will kill all caterpillars indiscriminately, so if you like butterflies, hold the poisons. Land development and environmental changes can disrupt their specific plant and habitat needs.

Butterflies serve an important role in the food chain; they are significant plant pollinators germinating the seeds of plants while gathering nectar, and they also are an important source of food for other insects and birds.

Grand Teton and Yellowstone National Parks display a wonderful variation of butterfly species, from the most widespread butterfly in the world, the Painted Lady, to Hayden's Ringlet and the Relict Fritillary, both unique to this small intermountain area that includes both parks.

Butterflies are insects in the order Lepidoptera. There are three subgroups: true butterflies (Papilionoidea), skippers (Hesperioidea), and moth butterflies (Hedyloidea). This guide covers the true butterflies and the skippers found in this area. The best general indicator to separate the subgroups is by the looking at the end of their antennae. True butterflies and skippers have knobbed antenna (with skippers the end is frequently also hooked). The moths lack a knob at the end of their antennae and have more variety in appearance, from a slender hair to a broad feather shape.

The butterfly has a magical life cycle, beginning with an egg usually laid on or near the larvae's host plant. Eggs are laid singly or in clusters numbering into the hundreds. The egg hatches into a larval caterpillar that will last multiple instars, or molts, as the caterpillar outgrows and sheds its skin and continues to feed on the host plant. The caterpillar will then enter a pupal or chrysalis stage during which metamorphosis occurs into the winged adult form. The average length of time from egg to adult is about a month, but it can vary in each stage and species. Adults can live from a week to almost a year, depending on the species. The Mourning Cloak, which over-winters in the adult stage, is the longest-lived species, surviving up to 10 – 12 months. Egg, larval and pupal stages may all have long periods of dormancy during which they over-winter or outlast harsh conditions.

Adults survive on liquids sucked through the proboscis, a long tube like structure, that is stored curled up between the labial palpi, or mouth parts. The proboscis extends when the butterfly senses the presence of food. Most butterflies will feed on nectar from flowers and minerals drawn from water in damp patches or mud puddles, although some species will prefer dung, rotting fruit, or sap. Butterflies have a unique sense of taste that is produced in the tarsi (feet), landing on plants to taste them or even scratching them to sense the plant type. The antennae are used to sense scent and chemical pheromones. Butterflies have compound eyes and well developed sight that is more sensitive to the ultraviolet spectrum of light than human vision. The wings of the butterfly are made rigid by the veins, and are composed of two membranous sheets covered with tiny overlapping scales, like the shingles on a roof. The color in the wings is created two different ways:

the earth tones and similar colors are from pigments, while the bright iridescent hues are created by refractions and reflections from the microstructure of the scales. The wing scales can also produce scent hormones for identification and to repel or attract other butterflies.

Adults display many interesting mating behaviors. They frequently perch in their chosen places, basking in the sun while waiting for a member of the opposite sex to pass by. They may also do some patrolling or flying about in an area in search of a mate. The males may defend their locations by chasing others that stray into the area, looping straight upward in chase before settling back to a perch. The differences in flight styles are a characteristic used to identify some species. Is the flight fast or slow, direct or bouncing, or flap and glide? Mating rituals can involve flight dances that can last several hours, and mating can occur while the pair is joined in flight.

Some species in this area, such as the Monarch or Painted Lady, are unable to survive the winter climate but migrate or emigrate from the south each summer season to repopulate the area. Others, such as the Commas and Tortoiseshells, will over-winter in adult form, surprising us with their appearance on the first warm days of spring.

This book is a photographic guide to assist with the enjoyment and identification of the butterflies found in the diverse ecosystems of Grand Teton and Yellowstone National Parks. The current census information has documented between 120 and 130 species in the area encompassing the two parks. Over one hundred living, free-flying species are pictured in this guide. Descriptions are provided for all the photographed species, with some additional descriptions for a few species that visit this area but are shown in illustrations. The butterflies are grouped by family and species. The descriptions provided include size (based on the distance between wingtips), identifying markings, similar species, and approximate flight time and general habitat. When a species exhibits polymorphism, or sexual variation in form, a photograph or documentation of the differences is included.

Some species, such as the Hesperis and Great Basin Fritillaries, are extremely difficult to identify by visual inspection, and others, like the Variable Checkerspot, exhibit many variations across a large number of subspecies. Even the experts are not always in agreement about species variations. For some species, little or nothing is known about some life stages or food sources. These behavioral observations offer opportunity for you to contribute to our knowledge of these fantastic insects.

Most butterflies can be easily observed if you approach with patience under the proper conditions and follow some simple reminders. They are cold-blooded insects that only fly when the temperature is near or above 60 degrees Fahrenheit and/or the sun is shining to warm them up. They are most active during the mid-morning to late afternoon hours. Some knowledge of habitat, host plants, and flowering plant or other food sources will assist you in finding specific species. The

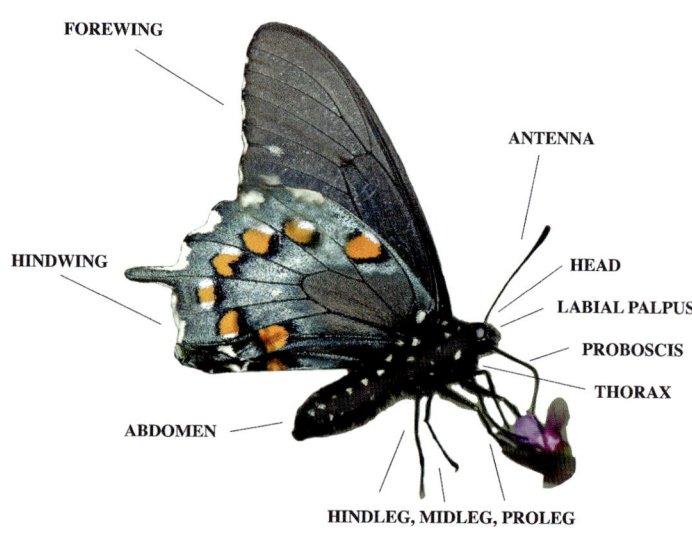

PARTS OF A BUTTERFLY

topographical variations in this area will also affect when and where you will see certain butterflies. Some prefer the high alpine environment and are only flying from mid-June to mid-August, while others can be found during the warm days in sheltered canyons on a southern exposure as early as March or as late as October. Our great seasonal variations in weather play an important role in our ability to find many species. Cool rainy summers will not produce the same species as a hot dry summer. Perhaps one of my favorite observing tips might be found in Paul Opler's book on Western Butterflies: "Stay low and go slow. Kneeling, sitting, or crawling, in combination with slow movements, will reward the observer." Don't forget your camera, but leave your net at home—the national parks encourage you to "take pictures but not specimens."

WING AREAS AND MARGINS

The two wings of the butterfly are composed of two chitinous sheets pressed together, they enclose veins running lengthwise and are covered with millions of tiny overlapping scales which may contain pigment or be faceted and reflect light to create hues.

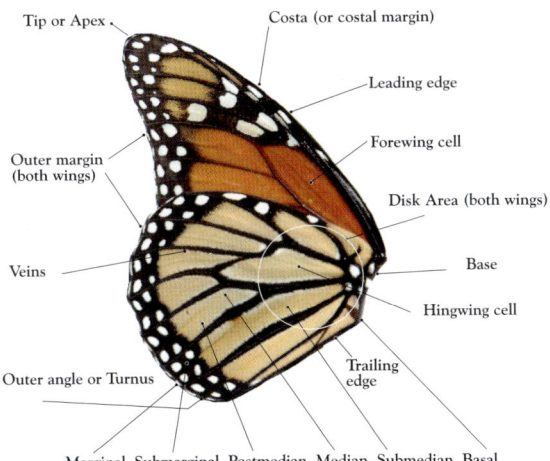

Tip or Apex
Costa (or costal margin)
Leading edge
Outer margin (both wings)
Forewing cell
Disk Area (both wings)
Veins
Base
Hingwing cell
Outer angle or Turnus
Trailing edge
Marginal, Submarginal, Postmedian, Median, Submedian, Basal

Clodius Parnassian

Parnassius clodius

IDENTIFICATION: Wing span 2 - 2½ inches. Upperside of forewing has three gray bars on leading margin and no red spots. Wings of both sexes translucent. Hindwing with red spots. Underside similar to upper but females have red at inner edge of hindwing. Mated females with prominent white pouch (sphragis) at end of abdomen that prevents additional matings. Similar to Rocky Mountain Parnassian which has red or black spots on forewing.

LIFE STAGES: Single egg laid on host plant. Caterpillar gray-black with short hair and a row of yellow or orange spots. Caterpillars are nocturnal and pupate in a silk wrap on the ground. Parnassians may be biennial with overwinter by egg and then pupae. Host plant the bleeding heart family. Adults sip nectar. Flight in June - July.

HABITAT: Forest meadows and rock outcrops, open woods.

No red on forewing

Underside coloration

CLODIUS PARNASSIAN

Rocky Mountain Parnassian

Parnassius smintheus

IDENTIFICATION: Wing span 1¾- 2½ inches. Distinguishing feature is alternating black and white rings on antennae. Upperside wings white with red and black markings. Two black bars on forewing leading edge darker, usually two red spots on forewing, more on hindwing. Red more extensive on female and on underside wings. Similar to Clodius Parnassian which lacks red on forewing and wings are more tranlucent. Rocky Mtn Parn. found at higher elevations.

LIFE STAGES: Single egg laid randomly. Caterpillar is black with short black hairs and yellow spots on sides. Host plant stonecrop. Adults fly low and nectar at flowers. Flight June - August.

HABITAT: Higher alpine environments, dry open tundra, rocky ridges.

Female parnassian

Male parnassian

Underside coloration

Pale Swallowtail

Papilio eurymedon

IDENTIFICATION: Wing span 2½ - 3¾ inches. Tiger striped black on white with slender black veins. Forewing pointed and narrower than hindwing. Hindwing tail long and twisted, orange and blue scales on hindwing base. Western Tiger Swallowtail is similar but yellow rather than white.

LIFE STAGES: Single chartreuse egg laid on host leaves. Caterpillar green with yellow-black eyespots on thoracic area. Caterpillar eats leaves and will make silk mat in curled leaves to rest. Host trees and shrubs in the cherry and ash familys. Adult males patrol hillsides and perch on knolls. Flight late April - July.

HABITAT: Conifer forest openings, hillsides, and streamsides.

On chockcherry blossom

Anise Swallowtail

Papilio zelicaon

IDENTIFICATION: Wing Span 2¼ - 3½ inches. Tailed with black veins. Abdomen black with yellow lateral stripe. Upperside forewing with yellow median band and two yellow bars on leading edge. Hindwing yellow with black submarginal area that has blue scaling and yellow or orange eyespot at anal angle with centered black spot. Underside pattern similar but cream rather than yellow. Similar to Old World Swallowtail which has a more yellow abdomen and eyespot center touches inner edge.

LIFE STAGES: Females lay single yellow egg on host leaves and flowers. Caterpillars eat host leaves and flowers. Caterpillar green with black band at each mid segment and rows of orange dots with each band. Host plants in our area in parsley family, particularly cow parsnip. Overwinters in chrysalid stage. Flight May - July.

HABITAT: Hillsides, mountains, fields, and gardens.

Indra Swallowtail

Papilio indra

IDENTIFICATION: Wing span 2½ - 3 inches. Mostly black. Short tails. Abdomen black with short yellow dash on side at end. Upperside and underside similar. Wings black, with pale-yellow postmedian band and yellow marginal spots, hindwing has blue iridecent spots and yellow eyespot with centered black spot. Similar to Black Swallowtail, black form of Anise Swallowtail and Old World Swallowtail. Many geographic variations of the Indra are found in the western U.S.

LIFE STAGES: Single egg laid on host leaves or flowers. Caterpillar is black with variable colors found as bands, white, yellow or orange. Host plants in the parsley family (Apiaceae). Chrysalis overwinters. Adult males perch on ridges awaiting females. Flight May - July.

HABITAT: Dry mountainous areas, preferring rocky ridgetops.

illustration by Emily Poole

Old World Swallowtail

Papilio machaon

IDENTIFICATION: Wing span 2½ - 3⅜ inches. Large black and yellow butterfly with variable subspecies. Distinguished from similar Anise swallowtail by the lack of a pupil in the hindwing red-orange tailspot, may have a black bar or rim at inner or lower margin of eyespot.

LIFE STAGES: Single egg laid on or near host plant. Caterpillar is green with orange or yellow spots and a black band on each segment. Host plants sagebrush (Artemisia), parsley family, and wormwood. Chrysalid will overwinter. Adults nectar at flowers and perch on hilltops. Flight June – July.

HABITAT: Forest edges, watercourses, brushy meadows.

Two-tailed Swallowtail

Papilio multicaudatus

IDENTIFICATION: Wing span 3 - 5¼ inches. Two tails on each hindwing. Upperside yellow with narrow black stripes on forewing, male has narrower stripe than female. Female may be more yellow or orange and have more blue iridescence on hingwing. Similar Tiger and Three-tailed Swallowtails have one and three tails respectively.

LIFE STAGES: Females lay single egg on host leaves. Caterpillar is green or brown with eyespots on thorax and two rows of blue spots extend down the body. Host plant, ash or chockcherry, leaves eaten by caterpillar which will make a silk shelter in curled leaves. Flight from May thru August. Adults sip nectar from many flower types.

HABITAT: Various, woodlands, moist openings and streamsides, roadsides and community gardens.

Western Tiger Swallowtail

Papilio rutulus

IDENTIFICATION: Wing span 2½ - 4 inches. Upper and undersides; yellow with black tiger stripes. Forewing, with yellow and black margin, hindwing, mostly yellow with black and blue submarginal band and two orange spots at anal angle. Similar species, Pale Swallowtail is pale white not yellow, Two-tailed Swallowtail has two tails.

LIFE STAGES: Single, shiny green, egg laid on host leaves. Caterpillar is light green with eyespots on thorax. Pupae hibernate. Host plants, willow, aspen, cottonwood and ash, among others. Adults gather in large groups at mud puddles. Flight June - July.

HABITAT: Forested areas with host plants, roadcuts, watercourses, and suburban gardens.

Desert Marble

Euchloe lotta

IDENTIFICATION: Wing span 1⅛ – 1⅜ inches. White butterfly with yellow green marbling on underside that is very similar to the Large Marble (see photo) also found in this area. There are two identifying characteristics, the white area on the underside hindwing has a pearly iridescence and the black bar on the forewing leading edge lacks white scaling.

LIFE STAGES: Single egg laid on host plant. Green larva has a white line on each side topped by a purple line. Caterpillar host plants in the mustard family notably rock cress (aribis), caterpillar prefers flowers and fruits. Adult males patrol ridges and hilltops. Flight April – May.

HABITAT: Open arid areas, rocky ridges, exposed slopes, and sagebrush meadows.

Large Marble

Euchloe ausonides

IDENTIFICATION: Wing span 1¼ - 2 inches. Upperside forewing white with black pattern at apex and black discal spot containing white scales. Underside, similar pattern on forewing but apex marking are yellow green; hindwing mostly white but marbled green with yellow veins extending thru green pattern. Similar to Desert marble which has no white scales in discal spot and more green than white on hindwing.

LIFE STAGES: Single egg laid on flower bud. Caterpillar blue-gray with black dots and yellow and white bands. Chrysalids hibernate. Host plants in mustard family. Adults nectar at flowers.

HABITAT: Forest openings, meadows, and watercourses, in foothills and canyons.

Becker's White

Pontia beckerii

IDENTIFICATION: Wingspan $1\frac{3}{8}$ - $1\frac{7}{8}$ inches. Upperside; white with squarish black patch in forewing cell, white scales in black patch. Some black markings on forewing tip around veins. Underside; hindwing with broad green borders on yellow veins, broken at outer edge of cell, creating a white median band, forewing has black cell spot and greenish wingtip markings. Similar to the Checkered White, Spring White, and Western White, none of these have white band on hindwing below.

LIFE STAGES: Single, spindle shaped, egg laid on host plant. Caterpillar pale green with raised black dots and orange bands. Host plants in the mustard and caper familys. Two flights, May - June and August - September.

HABITAT: Arid areas, sage flats, dry canyons and foothills, juniper woodlands.

Median white band on hindwing

Spring White

Pontia sisymbric

IDENTIFICATION: Wing span 1¼ - 1½ inches. Upperside; pale white with dark veins, narrow dark cell spot, and dark apex markings along veins. Underside, gray-brown pattern along veins on forewing tip and hindwing, yellow scaling on hindwing veins. Similar to Beckers White and Western White which are larger and have larger markings in forewing cells.

LIFE STAGES: Single yellow egg laid on host plant leaf. Caterpillar is yellow with wide black and white banding on each segment and a black head speckled with tiny white projections. Chrysalis hibernates. Host plants, mustard family, rock cress. Flight May - June.

HABITAT: Pine forests, dry hillsides, canyons and ridges.

Western White

Pontia occidentalis

IDENTIFICATION: Wing span 1½ - 2⅛ inches. White. Upperside of forewing with marginal black markings lighter in tone than marking in submarginal band. Black bar center of leading edge. Underside hindwing marks gray-green along veins. Darker marking on spring and fall forms. Very similar to Checkered White, hard to differentiate early season forms, summer form appears much whiter with only a few spots.

LIFE STAGES: Females lay single egg on host flower or leaf. Caterpillar blue-gray to green with alternating tone stripes and covered with black dots, head with yellow spots. Host plants in mustard family. Adults sip nectar from many flowers. Flight late May - August in our area.

HABITAT: Alpine slopes, meadows, forest openings including roadsides and streamsides.

Aster flower

Pine White

Neophasia menapia

Upperside coloration

IDENTIFICATION: Wing span 1¾ - 2 inches. Both wings white. Forewing with black costal margin and apex, black area at apex has white spots. Underside of hindwing has veins lined black, outline is more extensive on the female. Females also have red-orange color in margin and a black submarginal stripe. Similar Whites in our area, Checkered, Beckers, Western, and Spring, lack the black costal margin.

LIFE STAGES: Eggs laid in row on conifer needle to overwinter. Caterpillar is dark green with white stripe and wide white band. Caterpillars feed in trees but pupate on ground near base of tree.Host plants are pines and firs. Adults have floating flight high in trees but visit yellow composite flowers on ground to get nectar. Large outbreaks of this species may defoliate pine forests. Flight in June - September.

HABITAT: Conifer forests, forest openings.

Margined White

Pieris marginalis

IDENTIFICATION: Wing span 1⅜ - 2 inches. Upperside, may appear totally white to heavily striped on veins with black and 1 or 2 black spots in discal cell. Underside, may appear totally white but more often is marked with gray-green or yellow green along veins. Similar to Cabbage White which is usually darker at wing apex and not marked along veins.

LIFE STAGES: Eggs laid singly on underside of leaves. Caterpillar green with tiny black dots and faint light line on sides. Chrysalids hibernate. Host plants in the mustard family, including cresses. Adults nectar at flowers preferring the host plants.

HABITAT: Varies from moist areas and water courses to forest openings and meadows.

Underside coloration

Stella Orangetip

Anthocharis stella

IDENTIFICATION: Wing span 1 - 1⅞ inches. Upperside of male forewing with orange-red spot surrounded by black edging spots and narrow black bar at leading margin also broken dark border at apex. Males mostly white while females are pale yellow. Underside of hindwing marbled black-green. No similar species in this area.

LIFE STAGES: Single egg laid near top of host plant, caterpillars eat the flower buds, flowers and fruits. Chrysalids overwinter. Host plant is rockcress in mustard family. One flight May - July. Adults sip flower nectar, males patrol.

HABITAT: Open forests, fields and meadows, stream courses.

Queen Alexandra's Sulphur

Colias alexandra

IDENTIFICATION: Wing span 1½ - 2 inches. Upperside, yellow with narrow black border, usually absent or diminished in females. A green-white female version is possible. Underside, green-gray with hindwing white cell spot without rim. Similar to Western and Christina Sulphurs.

LIFE STAGES: Single egg laid on top of host plant leaf. Caterpillar green with white and yellow-orange stripe alternating along sides. Caterpillar will overwinter. Adults nectar at flowers. Host plant legumes and vetches. Flight May - September.

HABITAT: Prefers open spaces, meadows, sagebrush flats, and forest openings such as roadcuts.

Mead's Sulphur

Colias meadii

IDENTIFICATION: Wing span 1¼ - 2 inches. Fringes pink. Upperside, bright red-orange with wide black border; male with yellow spots in black border and a rimmed oval lighter patch on hindwing base. Underside, forewing yellow with wide green border, hindwing yellow-green to green with single pink rimmed discal spot. Rare white female form. Similar species in area, Orange Sulphur.

LIFE STAGES: Single egg laid on host leaves. Caterpillar yellow-green with black dots and pale yellow-white lateral stripes. Host plants legumes and clovers. Caterpillar overwinters. Adults nectar at flowers. Flight, brief period, in July - August.

HABITAT: High alpine meadows at or above treeline.

Pink-Edged Sulphur

Colias interior

IDENTIFICATION: Wing span 1¼ - 2 inches. Fringes bright pink. Upperside; male, yellow with narrow black border, narrower on hindwing, female black only at forewing tip or absent. Hindwing discal spot orange. Underside, yellow with single pink rimmed silver cell spot. Similar to Giant Sulphur and Pelidne Sulphurs.

LIFE STAGES: Single, pale, egg laid on host leaves. Caterpillar yellow-green with white stripes with red edges on sides. Caterpillar overwinters. Host plant Vaccinium family, huckleberry in this area. Flight June - August.

HABITAT: Open areas, scrubby forest and meadow edges, roadside mud puddles, burned areas.

Mud puddling

Pelidne Sulphur

Colias pelidne

IDENTIFICATION: Wing span 1¼ - 1½ inches. Pale yellow with pink fringes, female usually white. Upperside; black wing margin on male, fainter or absent on female, single small black cell spot. Underside; appears more olive colored with black scaling, small hindwing spot pink rimmed, may appear pink rather than white. Similar Pink-edged Sulphur is more yellow on underside with less black scaling.

LIFE STAGES: Not reported. Host plants blueberry (Vaccinium) or creeping wintergreen (Gaultheria) Flight late June - August.

HABITAT: Subalpine forest openings and meadows. Huckleberry heaths in both GTNP and YNP higher elevations are good places to find this species.

Clouded Sulphur

Colias philodice

IDENTIFICATION: Wing span 1⅜ - 2¼ inches. Pink fringes. Upperside; male, yellow with sharp black borders, female yellow or white with yellow spots within the black border. Underside; some submarginal dark spots, cell spot with two rings and usually a satellite spot. Similar to Orange Sulphur, which usually has orange on the upperside, and clear yellow lower not greenish.

LIFE STAGES: Single reddish egg laid on host leaf. Caterpillar smooth, green with dark stripe on back and light lateral stripes. Host plant legumes, prefering alfalfa and clovers. Flight May - October.

HABITAT: Very common butterfly. Open habitat, fields, meadows, and roadsides. Frequents mud puddles.

Male on left; female on right

Orange Sulphur

Colias eurytheme

IDENTIFICATION: Wing span 1½ - 2¾ inches. Variable. A very common butterfly. Wing fringe narrowly pink. Upperside some orange with broad black border, yellow veins, and dark black cell spot. Underside of forewing with some small black submarginal spots, hindwing has silver spot surrounded by two dark rings and spot above it. Similar to Clouded Sulphur which lacks orange upperside.

LIFE STAGES: Females lay eggs singly on top of host plant leaf, which caterpillar eats. Caterpillar is dark green with white and black stripe on side. The host plants, alfalfa, white clovers, and vetches, are very common and benefit the spread of this butterfly. Sulphur's may be considered a pest in alfalfa fields. Flight June - October.

HABITAT: Open areas, fields of host plants, meadows, and road edges.

Cloudless Sulphur

Phoebis sennae

IDENTIFICATION: Wing span 2½ - 3¼ inches. Large sulphur. Upperside, male, clear yellow, female may also have white form. Underside, spot in forewing cell, double silvered spots centered on hindwing. Scattered small sqiggles on both wings. Other large sulphurs rare in area.

LIFE STAGES: This butterfly is a tropical migant in this area. The host plant cassias, in the pea family, is not found here. This strong fast flyer may appear in the area in the warm summer days. It will nectar at long tubed flowers.

HABITAT: Prefers open areas, may be found in many habitats during it migrations.

Underside coloration

Rocky Mountain Dotted Blue

Euphilotes ancilla

IDENTIFICATION: Wing span ⅝ - 1 inch. Weakly checkered white fringe. Upperside male deep blue with medium to wide black borders, hingwing aurora usually missing. Female brown with blue near base, variable orange patch on hindwing. Thin terminal line. Underside of both sexes light blue gray with two rows of black spots and orange aurora on hindwing. Similar to Rocky Mtn. Square Dotted Blue, with is not found in Northwestern Wyoming.

LIFE STAGES: Eggs laid singly on flowers or buds. Caterpillars eat flowers and seeds and may be tended by ants. Favored host plant is Sulpher Buckwheat (Eriogonum). Adult Dotted Blues usually stay near host plant and feed on nectar. Chrysalids hibernate in leaf litter. One flight May - August.

HABITAT: Sunny rock slopes and meadows with host plants.

Spring Azure

Celastrina ladon

IDENTIFICATION: Wing span ⅞ - 1½ inches. Sexes differ. Upperside; males blue, females with black or gray on outer third of forewing and may have marginal spots on hindwing. Underside, gray white with black botches or spots and gray zigzig submarginal line. No similar species in our area, but this butterfly may be reclassified into more than one species in the western area.

LIFE STAGES: Eggs laid singly on flower buds. Caterpillar is usually green with red and or yellow on humps of back. Larvae are tended by ants, pupa hibernates. Host plants are woody shrubs and trees with white flowers such as dogwood, cherries, or serviceberries. Adults nectar at flowers. Flight, early spring, April - June.

HABITAT: Forest openings and roadcuts, usually near water courses, wooded swamps, and marshes.

Western Tailed-Blue

Everes amyntula

IDENTIFICATION: Wingspan ⅞ - 1⅛ inches. Narrow tail on hindwing. Upperside of male blue, female brown with blue at wing base. Underside white with black spots which may be indistinct. A single orange spot with blue center near tail.

LIFE STAGES: Eggs laid on flowers or seedpods of host plants, usually a legume such as lupine or milkvetch. Caterpillars eat the seeds and pupate in the pods to overwinter. Caterpillars are variable in color from green to yellow green sometimes marked with pink or maroon. Adults feed on flower nectar. Flight is May-July. No other tailed blues are found in our area.

HABITAT: Open areas in meadows and woodlands, as with most Blues, the males are frequent visiters to moist sand or mud.

Boisduval's Blue

Icaricia icarioides

IDENTIFICATION: Wing span 1 - 1⅜ inches. A widely variable butterfly. Upperside of male is lilac-blue with a relatively wide black submarginal area on both wings. Female varies from brown to blue with dark borders. Underside varies from brown to off white with two rows of black or white roundish spots on both wings. Postmedian spots are usually larger on forewing than hindwing. Hindwing spots are white in this population. Similar species, Silvery Blue and Greenish Blue.

LIFE STAGES: Eggs are laid on host plants, various Lupine species in the Pea family. Caterpillars green with white diaginal bars on each segment. Caterpillars feed on the leaves, flowers, and seedpods. The caterpillar produces a sugary secretion which is eaten by ants who serve a protective role for the caterpillars. Flight varies from early spring thru August. Adults feed on nectar from flowers.

HABITAT: Forest clearings and edges, meadows, sagebrush flats, and moist ground near watercourses.

Male

Underside coloration

BOISDUVAL'S BLUE

Lupine Blue

Icaricia lupini

IDENTIFICATION: Wing span $\frac{7}{8}$ - $1\frac{1}{8}$. Upperside male deep blue with wide dark margins with wide orange band at hindwing margin with black interior spot, some divided into seperate chevrons. Upperside of female brown, also with orange band. Underside off white with pattern of black spots, blue flecked orange and black spots on hindwing. No similar species in our area.

LIFE STAGES: Eggs laid singly on flowers of host plants. Caterpillar is green-gray with white bands. Host plants primarily wild buckwheat family (Eriogonum), some legumes. Sulpher buckwheat grows in sagebrush flats in western Wyoming. Adults sip flower nectar. Flight May - August.

HABITAT: Canyons, alpine slopes and meadows, rocky outcrops, sagebrush, and roadsides.

Male

Underside coloration

LUPINE BLUE

Shasta Blue

Icaricia shasta

IDENTIFICATION: Wing span ¾ - 1 inch. Upperside; male is violet blue with darker margin that is broken into dots on hindwing, female may be brown with wider marginal markings and some orange caps inwardly on hindwing spots. Both have a dark bar at end of forewing cell. Underside; gray-brown with black spots on forewing and brownish spots on hindwing, hindwing has iridescent blue-green spots capped inwardly with orange crescents then white arrows. Similar to Northern Blue and Lupine Blue both with more orange and lacking brown underside spots.

LIFE STAGES: Single egg laid on host plant. Caterpillar variable color, eats vetches, lupines, and clovers. Adult reported to be weak fliers, often very low to ground. Flight July - August.

HABITAT: High mountain meadows, rocky slopes, wideswept ridges and alpine streamsides.

Arrowhead Blue

Glaucopsyche piasus

IDENTIFICATION: Wingspan $\frac{7}{8}$ - $1\frac{1}{4}$. White fringe checkered black at vein ends. Upperside of both sexes dull blue, the female may be duller with variable orange on margins of wings. Underside gray with many white ringed black spots. Hindwing with postmedian white arrowheads pointing inward, may have some orange at base of the arrowhead. Similiar to Boisduval's Blue which lacks white arrowhead.

LIFE STAGES: Pale egg laid on flowers of host plants, prefering lupines and milk vetches. The caterpillar is variable in color, blue-green to yellow-brown with tiny speck of red or white. a dark band on the back and sides. The caterpillar will eat the host flowers and seeds. Adult males will patrol near host plants and feed on nectar from flowers. Flight in April to July.

HABITAT: Open meadows, sagebrush flats, roadsides and streamsides.

Unusual black spot in hingwing center

Silvery Blue

Glaucopsyche lygdamus

IDENTIFICATION: Wing span ⅞ - 1¼ inches. Upperside both wings with a black margin and white fringe. Male is irridescent silvery blue, female darker brown or blue. Underside is off white to gray brown with a single row of white ringed black spots. Similar to Boisduval's Blue and Greenish Blue.

LIFE STAGES: Eggs laid singly on flower buds and leaves of host plants. Caterpiller varies from green to purple with a dark stripe and white lateral lines. Caterpillars are tended by ants. Host plants include Vetches, Lupines, and other species in the pea family.

HABITAT: Open areas including mountain meadows, foothills, grasslands, road edges, bogs and moist areas at water course edges.

REMARKS: A subspecies once found in the sand dunes of San Francisco, the Xerces Blue, is extinct. The Xerces Society, an invertebrate conservation organization, takes its name from this butterfly. Another subspecies, the Palo Verdes Blue, is also very near extinction.

Photographed on Specimen Ridge, YNP

Melissa Blue

Lycaeides melissa

IDENTIFICATION: Wing span ⅞ - 1⅜. This is the most common blue in the intermountain region. Sexes differ. Upperside of male is blue with narrow dark border. Female is brown, sometimes with mostly blue near base of wing, with submarinal orange trim with black spot on both wings. Underside white with black spots and continuous black line on outer margin of both wings, also orange submarginal spots on both wings. Similiar species in area is Northern Blue which has broken marginal line.

LIFE STAGES: Eggs are laid on host plants or nearby. Caterpillars are hairy green with darker green stripe on back and lighter stripe on sides. Caterpillar tended by ants. Host plant legumes including alfalfa, lupines and clovers. Three flights from April - October.

HABITAT: Open areas, meadows, alfalfa fields, and weedy areas.

Northern Blue

Lycaeides idas

IDENTIFICATION: Wing span ¾ - 1¼ inches. Sexes varied. Upperside; male blue with narrow black marginal line, female brown tinged with blue, orange submarginal spots. Underside, both pale gray with black spots, a marginal row of black spots, both wings and metallic blue spots capped orange and black. Distinguishing feature is thin black submarginal line broken into spots on hindwing. Similar to Melissa Blue which has continuous thin black submarginal line and larger orange spots.

LIFE STAGES: Not well documented. Host plants in pea family, lupines and vetches. Flight June - August.

HABITAT: High alpine tundra, wet meadows, openings in evergreen forests.

Spotted hindwing submarinal line

Female

NORTHERN BLUE

Greenish Blue

Plebejus saepiolus

IDENTIFICATION: Wing span 1 - 1¼ inches. Sexes differ. Upperside; male, metallic blue with row of pale black spots on margin of hindwing; female light brown, hindwing spots may be orange capped. Underside, male is silver-gray and female grey or tan, both with two rows of black spots on both wings, partial third row capped with orange on male hindwing. Similar to Boisduvals and Silvery blues.

LIFE STAGES: Single egg laid on host flowers. Caterpillar has two color forms, red and green. Host plant various clovers, perhaps milkvetches. Flight May - August.

HABITAT: Open areas with clover, moist areas, roadsides, and watercourses.

Mating pair

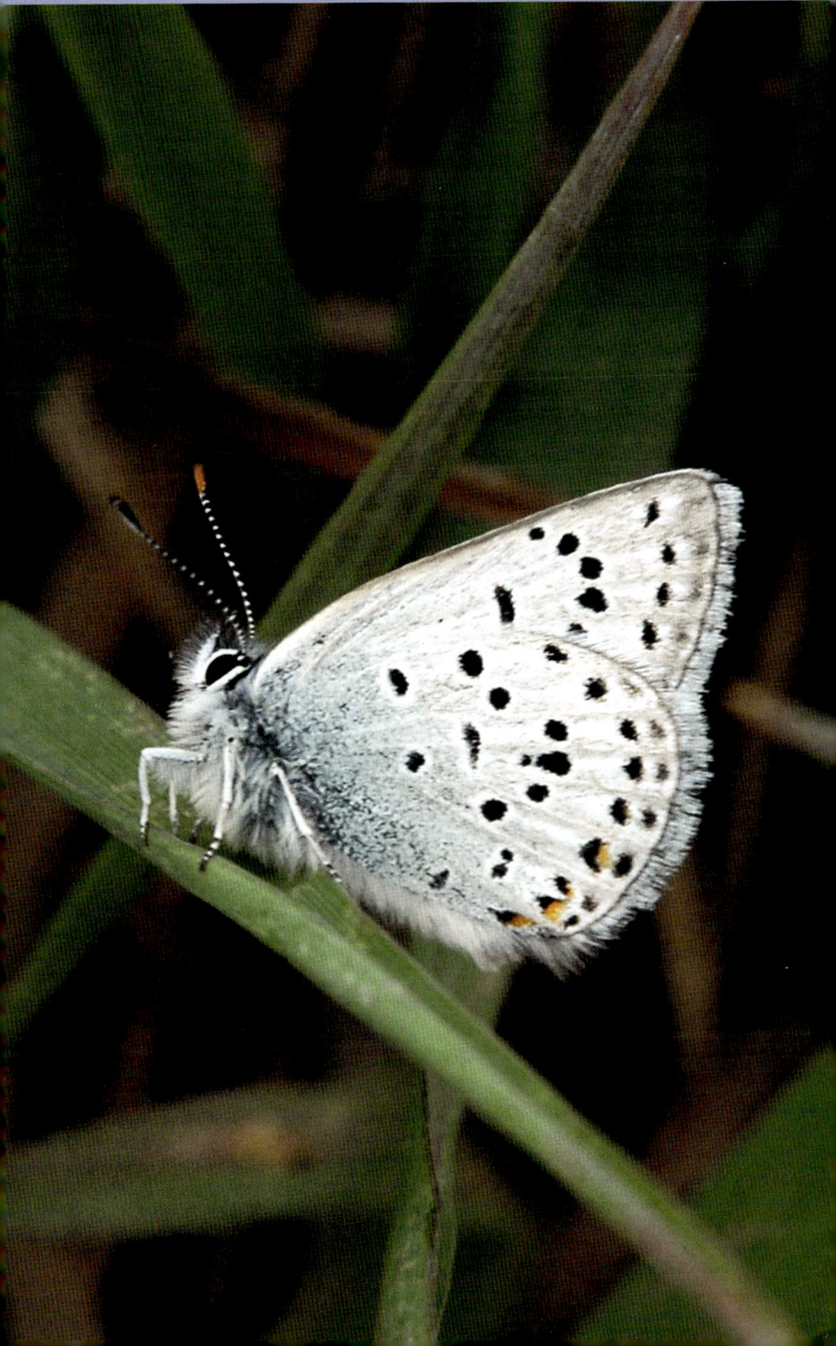

Blue Copper
Lycaena heteronea

IDENTIFICATION: Wing span 1 - 1 $^{5}/_{16}$ inches. Upperside black border with white fringe. Males bright blue, female gray sometimes with blue or brown with dark spots. Underside white to off whites with dark spot on forewing, hindwing sometimes with spots. Similar to Boisduval's Blue.

LIFE STAGES: Eggs laid on underside of host leaves and hatch in the spring. Caterpillar gray-green with white hairs, yellow dashes on sides and dark stripe on back. Host wild buckwheats. Males patrol. Flight May - August.

HABITAT: Mountain valleys. open meadows, sagebrush.

Underside

Male

Female

BLUE COPPER

Mariposa Copper

Lycaena mariposa

IDENTIFICATION: Wing span 1⅛ - 1¼ inches. Black and white checkered fringe. Upperside brown, male iridescent purple with black borders and faint black marking, female black spots with yellow-orange patches on forewing. Underside forewing yellow with black spots, hindwing gray with black mottled cresent marks.

LIFE STAGES: Eggs laid near host will overwinter until spring. Caterpillar not reported. Host plant may be huckleberry, whortleberry, or wintergreen in heath family. Adults sip nectar. Males perch. Flight July - August.

HABITAT: Forest openings, streamsides, and lakeshores, near host plants.

Plain brown male above

Underside

Female

Male

Purplish Copper

Lycaena helloides

IDENTIFICATION: Wing span 1⅛ - 1½ inches. In our region this butterfly is extremely variable, may resemble Dorcas Copper found in Canada. Sexes differ in color and pattern. Upperside both sexes brown, male with purple iridescence, female with more orange areas on both wings. Orange zig-zag on hindwing on both sexes. Underside lighter yellow-orange or light brown both wings and black spots on forewing. Hindwing with smaller black spots and orange submarginal marking.

LIFE STAGES: Eggs laid in litter at base of host. After overwintering as egg caterpillar eats leaves in spring. Caterpillar green with white hairs and oblique yellow lines. Host plants, buckwheats, cinquefoils, and knotweeds. Adults sip nectar. Flight late June - August.

HABITAT: Wetlands, streamcourses, disturbed areas, roadsides, and fields.

Underside coloration

PURPLISH COPPER   61

Ruddy Copper

Lycaena rubidus

IDENTIFICATION: Wing span 1⅛ - 1½ inches. Sexes differ. Male upperside bright red orange or copper, female brown to orange with orange zigzag marginal band on hindwing. Underside of both sexes pale white to gray with prominent black spots on forewing, may have small diffuse black spots on hindwing. Female Blue Copper similar to female Ruddy, former lacks orange zigzag on upper hindwing. and has larger black spots on lower hindwing.

LIFE STAGES: Eggs laid singly at base of host plant, eggs hibernate and may be tended by ants. Host plants docks and buckwheats. Caterpillar brown with red stripe on back. Males perch and chase other males while awaiting females. Adults sip flower nectar. Flight July thru August.

HABITAT: Sand or gravel near water courses. Found at higher elevations in our area.

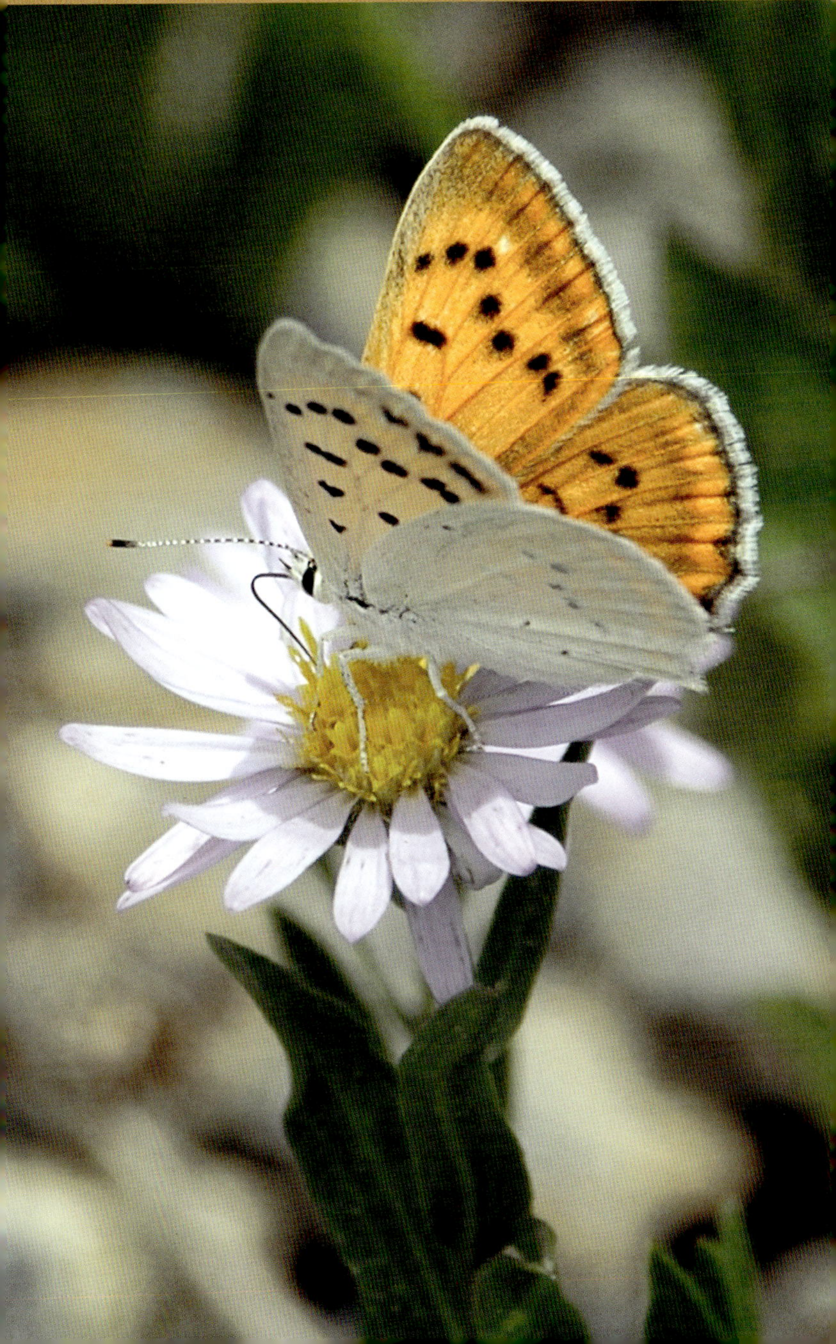

Lustrous Copper

Lycaena cuprea

IDENTIFICATION: Wing span 1 – 1¼ inches. Upperside; lustrous coppery red-orange, with black spots and black border. Female and higher altitude forms may be darker. Underside; gray forewing has orange tint with white outlined black spots, hindwing gray with numerous black spots and narrow orange submarginal stripe. Similar to Ruddy Copper which has fewer spots on upperside and a clear hindwing on underside.

LIFE STAGES: Not well documented. Eggs laid on host dock plants in some areas, host in this area may be mountain sorrel (*Oxyria digyna*). Caterpillar is light green with a red stripe on sides and red flecks on back. Flight July – August.

HABITAT: High mountain altitudes, meadows, talus slopes, and rocky streambeds.

(left) Upperside; (right) Underside

Bronze Copper

Lycaena hyllus

IDENTIFICATION: Wing span 1¼ - 1½ inches, larger than most other coppers. Upperside; Sexes differ, male copper-brown with iridescent violet sheen and orange hindwing marginal band, female forewing orange with black spots and margin, hindwing gray with dark spots and orange marginal band. Underside; both have orange forewing with dark spots and whitish hindwing with spots and orange marginal band. Similar to Purplish Copper that has zig-zag marginal bands.

LIFE STAGES: Single egg laid on plant will hibernate until spring. Caterpillar is yellow-green with dark line on back. Host plants docks (Rumex) and knotweeds (Polygonum). Adults perch, do not stray far from host plants. Flight June – August.

HABITAT: Open moist spaces such as marsh edges, wet meadows, and small watercourses where host plant is found.

Lilac-Bordered Copper

Lycaena nivalis

IDENTIFICATION: Wing span 1 - 1¼ inches. Upperside, male orange brown with lilac sheen, female brown with variable yellow orange. Both with black spots and orange zigzag band on hindwing margin. Underside, cream yellow with outer hindwing pink, perhaps the best distinguishing feature of this species. The pink and lilac shading fades quickly with age and appears dingy. Purplish copper similar species but lacks underside hindwing pink.

LIFE STAGES: Host plant knotweeds. Eggs laid singly on base of host and hibernate. Caterpillar green with a single red stripe and two white stripes on back. Adults nectar at flowers, males perch to await females. Flight in June - August.

HABITAT: Alpine meadows, forest clearings and roadcuts, sage flats, near water courses.

Compare hindwing with Purplish Copper

Edith's Copper

Lycaena editha

IDENTIFICATION: Wing span ⅞ - 1 ¼ inches. Sometimes with minute tail projecting from lower hindwing. Upperside; gray to gray-brown, male uniform color except for small black spot on some forewings, female with variable black spots with yellow base may also have orange margin on hindwing base. Underside; light gray with black spots on forewing, hindwing with complex gray mottled spots, with or without white backing, and sometimes orange submarginal marking.

LIFE STAGES: Little found in research of early stages. May overwinter in egg stage. Caterpillar not reported. Males may interact aggressively with other males while patrolling. Host plants knotweeds, buckwheats, cinquefoils, and gooseberries. Adults sip flower nectar. Flight June - August.

HABITAT: Openings in lodgepole forests, sagebrush flats, meadows, and streamsides.

(left) Female; (right) Male

Note the variation in the hindwings

EDITH'S COPPER

American Copper

Lycaena phlaeas

IDENTIFICATION: Wing span $\frac{7}{8}$ - $1\frac{3}{8}$ inches. Upperside; forewing bright red-orange with black spots and brown wing margin, hindwing brown with red-orange marginal band. Underside; FW orange with black spots and gray margin, HW gray with narrow orange submarginal zig zag line, small black spots. Similar to female Bronze Copper which is larger. See also Ruddy and Lustrous Coppers.

LIFE STAGES: Single green egg laid on host plant, probably Sheep sorrel (*Rumex acetosella*) in our area. Caterpillar variable, green with red side marks or red with yellow side marking, covered with downy hairs. Caterpillar will make channels in host leaves. Overwinters as chrysalis. Flight July - August.

HABITAT: Above treeline on open rocky slopes.

(opposite) Tattered wing of a Purplish Copper reveals the beak shape of an attacking bird.

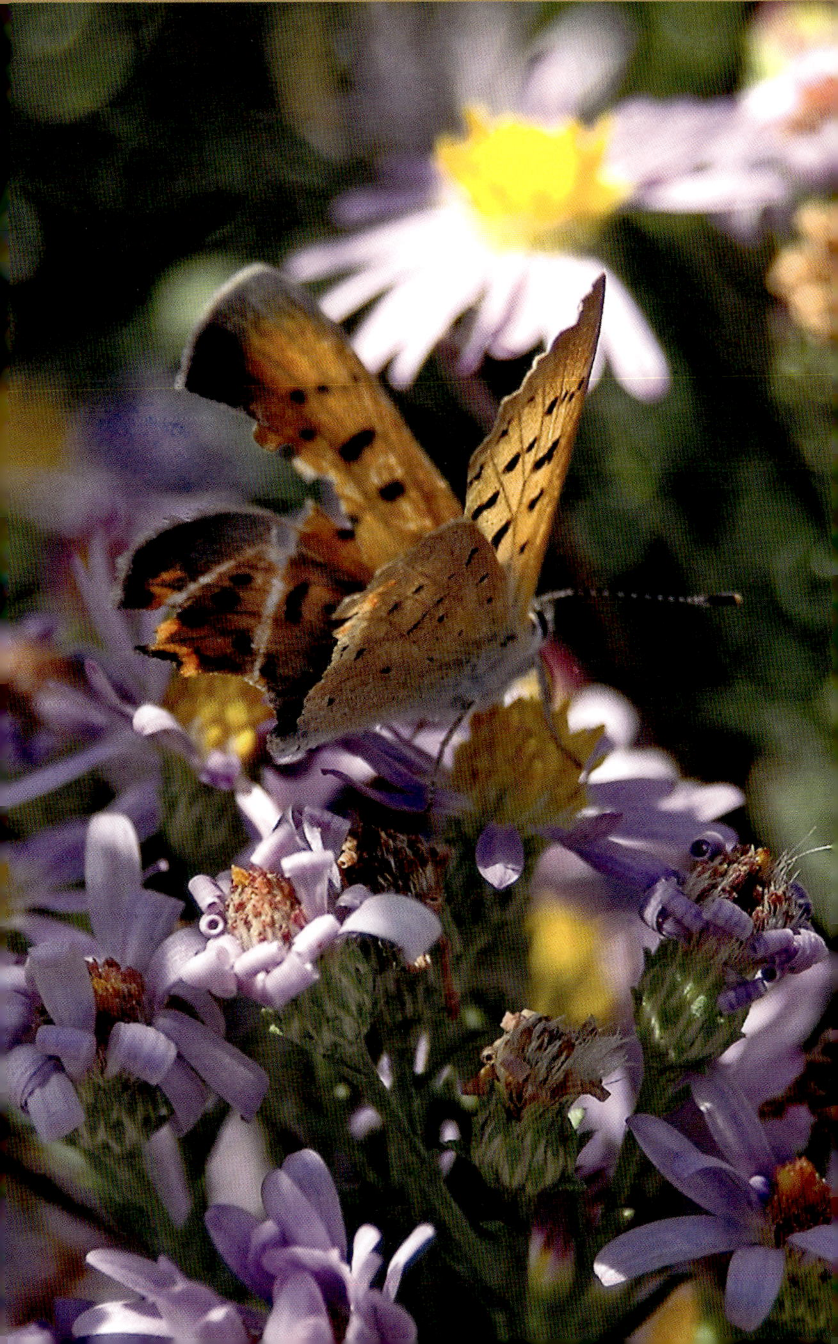

Brown Elfin

Callophrys augustinus

IDENTIFICATION: Wing span ¾ - 1 inch. Tailless. Upperside, plain gray/brown in male; female may have more orange. Underside, chestnut brown on outerside and dark brown on basal side, dark postmedian line and small submarginal spots. Similar species, Hoary Elfin and Moss Elfin may appear in some parts of this area.

LIFE STAGES: Eggs laid singly on host plant flowers. Caterpillar green with yellow dorsal stripe and lateral lines. Chrysalids hibernate. Host plants in heath family, bearberry, huckleberry, and Labrador tea. Adults perch, sip flower nectar and moisture from wet sand and earth. Flight April - June.

HABITAT: Wide variety of habitats, prefering acidic soils and areas with host plants in conifer forest.

Western Pine Elfin

Callophrys eryphon

IDENTIFICATION: Wing span ⅞ - 1¼ inches. Sexes similar. Tailless. Upperside reddish brown, lighter on female. Underside, forewing light brown with black and white marginal stripe, black submarginal chevrons. Fringes darker at vein endings. Hindwing, jagged dark brown bands outlined with thin white stripe. Purplish tone to lighter spots and bands. Zigzag band of submarginal chevrons black, brown, and white. No similar species in this area.

LIFE STAGES: Eggs laid on pine needles, caterpillar feeds on needles. Caterpillar is pine green with two light stripes running lenghtwise. Chrysalids hibernate. Host plant in our area is the young lodgepole pine. Males will perch on small trees to find females. Adults sip flower nectar.

HABITAT: Pine forest with young trees.

Underside coloration

Juniper Hairstreak

Callophrys gryneus

IDENTIFICATION: Wing span ⅞ -
1⅛ inches. Variable across range.
Upperside, red-brown to rust-brown
with darker edges. Underside; forewing
green at base and tip otherwise red-
brown with white postmedian line.
Hindwing green with irregular
postmedian white line edged inwardly
with brown, dark spots near tails. No
similar species in our area.

LIFE STAGES: Single green egg laid on tip of juniper leaves.
Caterpillar green with irregular surface and white or yellow bars
on sides. Chrysalis overwinters. Host plants juniper and cedar.
Adults nectar at flowers. Flight May - July.

HABITAT: Open, arid, scrub woodlands, canyons and hillsides,
with host juniper.

Western Green Hairstreak

Callophrys affinis

IDENTIFICATION: Wing span ¾ - 1⅛ inches. Tailless. Upperside gray to brown. Underside: green sometimes with a few white spots in marginal area. Similar to Sheridan's Hairstreak which has a strong marginal line and flies earlier.

LIFE STAGES: Eggs laid on Sulphur flower (*Eriogonum umbellatum*). Caterpillar varies from green to red with white lines on sides and back. Difficult to observe, wary, and fast strong flier. Flight May - June.

HABITAT: Near food plant in sagebrush, meadows, and sunny open hillsides.

Sheridan's Hairstreak

Callophrys sheridanii

IDENTIFICATION: Wing span ⅞ - 1 inch. No tail. Upperside gray- brown. Underside, bright green fading to brown with a median white line on both wings. Fringe's white and may also have white spot(s) on underside. Similar to Western Green Hairstreak which lacks the white line and is larger.

LIFE STAGES: Egg laid singly on host leaf. Caterpillar varies from green tones to pink color with white stripes on back and sides. Host plant buckwheats. Adults nectar at flowers. Flight April - June.

HABITAT: Open slopes, sagebrush, and sunny hillsides in canyons.

Faded coloration

Thicket Hairstreak

Callophrys spinetorum

IDENTIFICATION: Wing span ⅞ - 1 ¼ inches. Tailed. Upperside steel blue with difuse dark margins. Underside; red-brown with black and white postmedian line on both wings. Line has W shape near tail. Black spots on submarginal hindwing with some orange and blue scaling near tails. No similar species in area.

LIFE STAGES: Single egg laid on mistletoe. Caterpillar green with olive stripe on back and red, yellow, and white on ridges down segments. Host dwarf mistletoe, a parasite on conifers. Flight late April thru June. Adult perch on tree tops, sip nectar at flowers and moisture at wet areas.

HABITAT: Conifer forest, and forest opening and roadcuts.

(opposite) Broken wing with upperside exposed

Hedgerow Hairstreak

Satyrium saepium

IDENTIFICATION: Wing span ⅞ - 1¼ inches. Short tail. Upperside, bright copper brown. Underside, tan to dull brown with a faint dark irregular postmedian band, faint submarginal chevrons and a blue tailspot. Similar species in this area Behr's Hairstreak has an orange tailspot and diffuse white scaling underneath.

LIFE STAGES: Single egg laid on host plant. Egg hibernates. Caterpillar is light green with very short golden fuzz and white-yellow lateral stripe grows to ½ inch. Host plant buckbrush and snowbrush (Ceanothus). Adults nectar at flowers. Flight May thru August.

HABITAT: Dry mountain slopes and ridges near forest or brush.

Behr's Hairstreak

Satyrium behrii

IDENTIFICATION: Wing span 1 - 1⅛ inches. No tail. Upperside, orange-brown with broad brown-black margins on forewing. Underside, gray or gray-brown with two rows of black spots and dashes. Hindwing has one orange spot at anal angle. Similar species, Hedgerow Hairstreak which has a tail and blue spot.

LIFE STAGES: Eggs laid singly on leaves or twigs of host plants. Eggs hibernate. Caterpillar is green with white dorsal stripe and yellow and white lateral lines. Host plants rose family, probably antelope bitterbrush in this area. Adults nectar at flowers, males perch. Flight June - August.

HABITAT: Dryer locales with sage or antelope brush, ridgecrests.

Compare to Hedgerow Hairstreak

California Hairstreak

Satyrium californica

IDENTIFICATION: Wing span 1 - 1¼ inches. Tails. Upperside pale gray-brown with orange spot near tails. Underside; gray to brown with black spots and orange submarginal chevrons on hindwing, blue scaling near tail. Similar to Sylvan Hairstreak which is lighter underneath and has fewer orange spots.

LIFE STAGES: 2 - 4 eggs laid together in bark. Egg overwinters. Caterpillar is brown with gray patches and white chevrons on sides. Host plant in this area snowbrush (Ceanothus), perhaps scrub oaks. Flight June - July.

HABITAT: Lower elevation dry hillside openings with scrub brush and host plants.

Sooty Hairstreak

Satyrium fuliginosum

IDENTIFICATION: Wing span ⅞ - 1¼ inches. No tail. Rounded wings. Upperside brown to sooty black with no markings. Underside; gray to brown, 1 or 2 rows of postmedian black spots, and a single discal bar, that are frequently covered by white scales. Similar to female blues, Boisduval's Blue in particular.

LIFE STAGES: Single egg laid on or near host plant. Host lupine. Caterpillar not recorded. Adults nectar at flowers and males patrol lupine for females. Flight June - July.

HABITAT: Pine meadows, sagebrush, scree fields, ridges, and roadcuts.

Underside coloration

Sylvan Hairstreak

Satyrium sylvinus

IDENTIFICATION: Wing span ⅞ - 1⅜ inches. Tailed in our area. Upperside, Brown-gray with orange patch on hindwing margin. Underside; silver-gray with postmedian row of small black spots, discal bars. Hindwing blue spot at anal angle, black submarginal chevrons, some with orange cap. Similar to California Hairstreak which is browner below with more orange.

LIFE STAGES: Single egg laid on stems, egg hibernates. Caterpillar light green with white stripes on back and white dashes on sides. Host plant willows. Flight June - July.

HABITAT: Willow thickets, watercourses, forest openings. ridgelines.

Less orange than California Hairstreak

Gray Hairstreak

Strymon melinus

IDENTIFICATION: Wing span ⅞ - 1¼ inches. Most widespread hairstreak. Upperside; slate-gray with large orange spot above tail. Underside; lighter gray with post median, black lined, white line on both wings, edged inside with orange on hindwing. Large orange spot at tails has black spot at margin with tail. Orange-black spot at anal angle may have some blue scaling above. No similar species in this area.

LIFE STAGES: Single egg laid on host flower. Caterpillar variable green shades with white to purple lateral stripes. Caterpillar can be pest on hop, cotton, and bean crops. Hosts in pea (Fabaceae) and mallow (Malvacaeae) families. Flight May - August.

HABITAT: Open areas in a large range of habitat, meadows, sage, forest edges, and roadsides with host plants, not at high elevation in our area.

Coral Hairstreak

Satyrium titus

IDENTIFICATION: Wing span $\frac{7}{8}$ - $1\frac{1}{4}$ inches. No tail. Upperside is dark brown. Underside, brown with row of coral submarginal spots on hindwing, small black spots surrounded by white in postmedian row. Similar brown hairstreaks lack coral spots.

LIFE STAGES: Single egg laid on hostplant or at base in litter. Eggs hibernate. Caterpillar is covered in downy hairs, yellow green with red blotches at front and rear, black head. Host plants in rose family, probably chockcherry in this area. Adults are rapid fliers, nectar at flowers. Flight May - August.

HABITAT: Open meadows, roadcuts, forest openings, shrubby or bushy areas, and streamsides.

Zerene Fritillary

Speyeria zerene

IDENTIFICATION: Wing span 2 - 2¾ inches. Upperside variable across range, intermountain population paler with less black than some. Surface red-orange to red-brown with variable black markings. Underside paler yellow-brown with postmedian silver spots round to elongated and brown caps. Submarginal spots rounded with brown caps. Similar to Coronis which has rounder postmedian spots and never red above, also Hydaspe which is smaller and has rounder spots on underside.

LIFE STAGES: Eggs laid on ground litter near host violets. Caterpillar orange to tan with black-gray marking at base of spines. First stage caterpillar will overwinter and feed on leaves of violet in spring. Flight June - August.

HABITAT: Open conifer forest, lakeshore, and sagebrush meadows.

(right) Unusually silvered fritillary

Callippe Fritillary

Speyeria callippe

IDENTIFICATION: Wing span 2 - 2½ inches. Upperside variable, tawny to bright orange-brown with evenly spaced marking, sometimes black scaling. Silver spots show through as paler than surrounding color. Underside with triangular silver submarginal spots with narrow green edging. Background color variable from pale green to deep blue green or red-brown with no submarginal band. Similar to Edwards and Coronis Fritillarys.

LIFE STAGES: Eggs laid singly on ground near host plant, violets. Caterpillar is mottled gray-black with gray bands, many orange black spines. Caterpillars hibernate and feed on young violet leaves in spring. Flight May - August.

HABITAT: Various, grassland, sagebrush, brushy hillsides.

Mormon Fritillary

Speyeria mormonia

IDENTIFICATION: Wing span 1⅝ - 2 inches. Forewing rounded. Upperside; orange-brown with veins not usually blackened. Black markings slightly smaller than similar frits, female with wider black border. Underside; forewing base orange, similar pattern as upperside, disk variable red, brown, or tan but usually greenish. Hindwing spots smaller, with wider submarginal band than similar fritillarys. Similar Great Basin Frit has larger spots, Callippe Frit is more solid green, both with darker upperside veins.

LIFE STAGES: Egg laid near host, violets. Caterpillar gray or tan brown with spines and black stripes. Adults nectar at flowers. Flight June - September.

HABITAT: Mountain meadows, forest openings, sage flats.

Wide submarginal band

Coronis Fritillary

Speyeria coronis

IDENTIFICATION: Wing span 2 - 3 inches. Upperside orange to orange-brown with black bars. Marginal and postmedian spots may be paler than surrounding color. Underside hindwing with silvered spots, marginal row rounded inward or flattened and capped greenish brown or brown. Similar to Zerene Fritillary, sometimes impossible to separate when viewing in field. Zerene postmedian spots more elongated with rounded marginal spots capped brown.

LIFE STAGES: Eggs laid singly in duff near violets, laying may be delayed to late summer then the caterpillar will overwinter before feeding on violets in spring. The caterpillar is mottled brown-black with orange and black spines. Adults feed on flower nectar. Flight from June to September.

HABITAT: A wide variety including, mountain slopes, conifer forest, meadows and openings, and sagebrush flats.

Hydaspe Fritillary

Speyeria hydaspe

IDENTIFICATION: Wing span 1¾ - 2½ inches. Upperside, rich orange brown, darker at base, heavy dark pattern. Underside, maroon-brown or reddish with cream colored black ringed spots that are more square in shape. Dark distinctive hindwing color different than other frits.

LIFE STAGES: Single egg laid near host plant. Caterpillar hibernates before eating. Caterpillar black with black spines on back and yellow spines on sides. Host plant violets. Adult nectars at flowers. Flight June - August.

HABITAT: Forest openings, moist areas, watercourses.

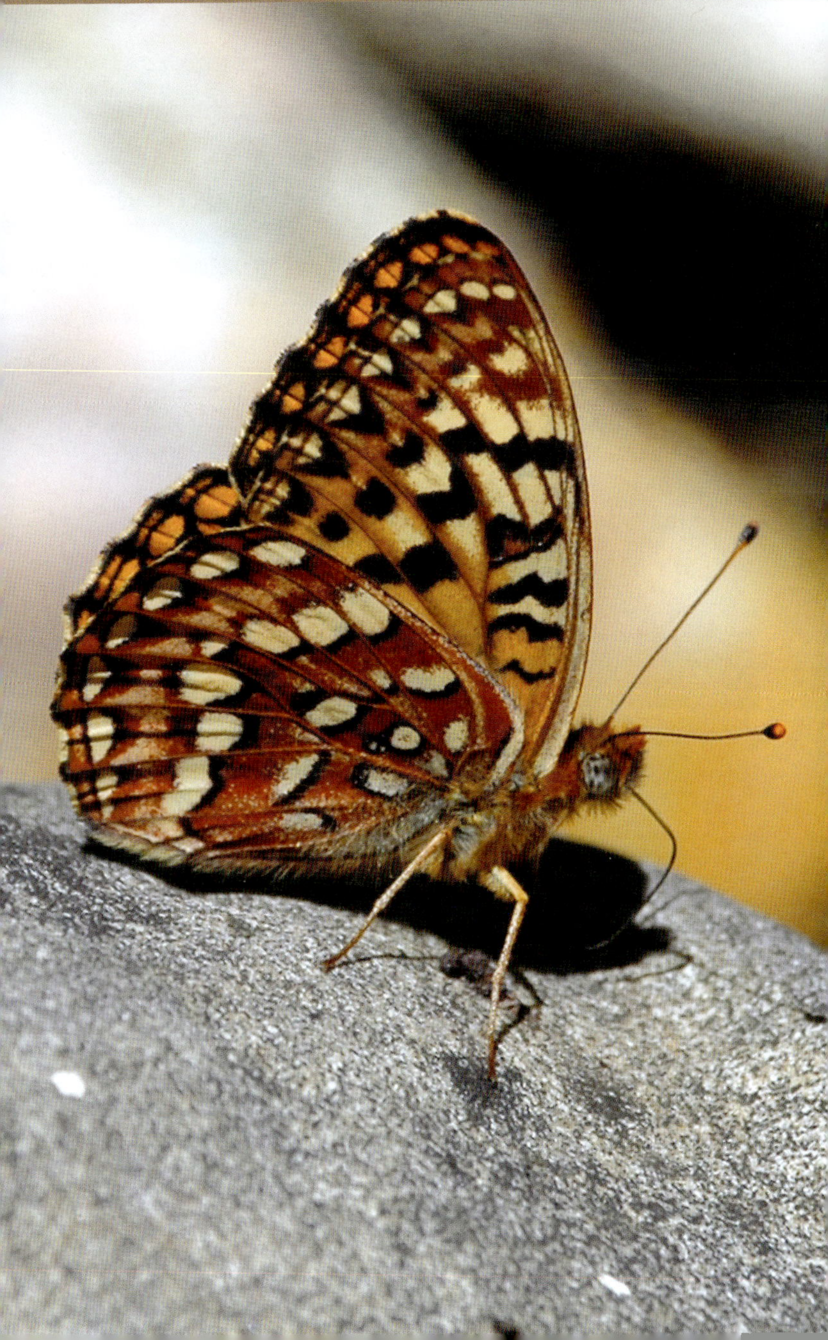

Great Spangled Fritillary

Speyeria cybele

IDENTIFICATION: Wing span 2½ - 3¾ inches. Largest fritillary in our area. Sexes varied. Male bright orange with black scaling on forewing veins and broad orange submarginal band on underside. Female yellow or white with black basal/medial area on both wings, also black marginal band. No similar large fritillaries in our area.

LIFE STAGES: Eggs laid on or near to host violet plants. Caterpillar is black with spines red at base. Caterpillar will overwinter and feed on young violets. Adults strong fast fliers, may fly in groups. Adults nectar at a wide variety of flowers. Flight June - September.

HABITAT: Forest edges and openings, meadows, along streamcourses and road cuts.

Female

Aphrodite Fritillary

Speyeria aphrodite

IDENTIFICATION: Wing span 2 - 3 inches. Variable. Amber colored eyes, similar species all with grey colored eyes except larger Great Spangled Fritillary. Upperside; male with small black spot below forewing cell, forewing veins without heavy black scales. Hindwing submarginal band narrow or absent. Bulls eye spot in submarginal band below silver spot. Similar to Northwestern and Great Basin Fritillaries, both smaller. Great Spangled Fritillary is larger.

LIFE STAGES: Single egg laid near host plant, violets. Caterpillar dark brown with black stripes and orange sides. Caterpillar overwinters. Adults nectar at flowers. Flight June - August.

HABITAT: Forest openings, meadows and foothills.

Amber colored eye

Northwestern Fritillary

Speyeria hesperis

IDENTIFICATION: Wing span 2 - 2¾ inches. Variable. Upperside; orange-brown with black outer margins, especially on forewing, often with dark scaling at base. Male with dark scaling on veins. Underside of hindwing red-brown to orange-brown basal disk with pale submarginal band, spots silvered or unsilvered. Similar to Atlantis Fritillary, which is not found in our area. Great Basin Fritillary hard to differentiate, hindwing disk may be paler.

LIFE STAGES: One egg is laid on leaf litter near violet host plant. The caterpillar is black with two brown lines on back and black tips to orange spines. Unfed caterpillar will overwinter. Adults fond of flower nectar from mints and yellow composites. Flight from June to September.

HABITAT: Forest openings, moist meadows, and open slopes.

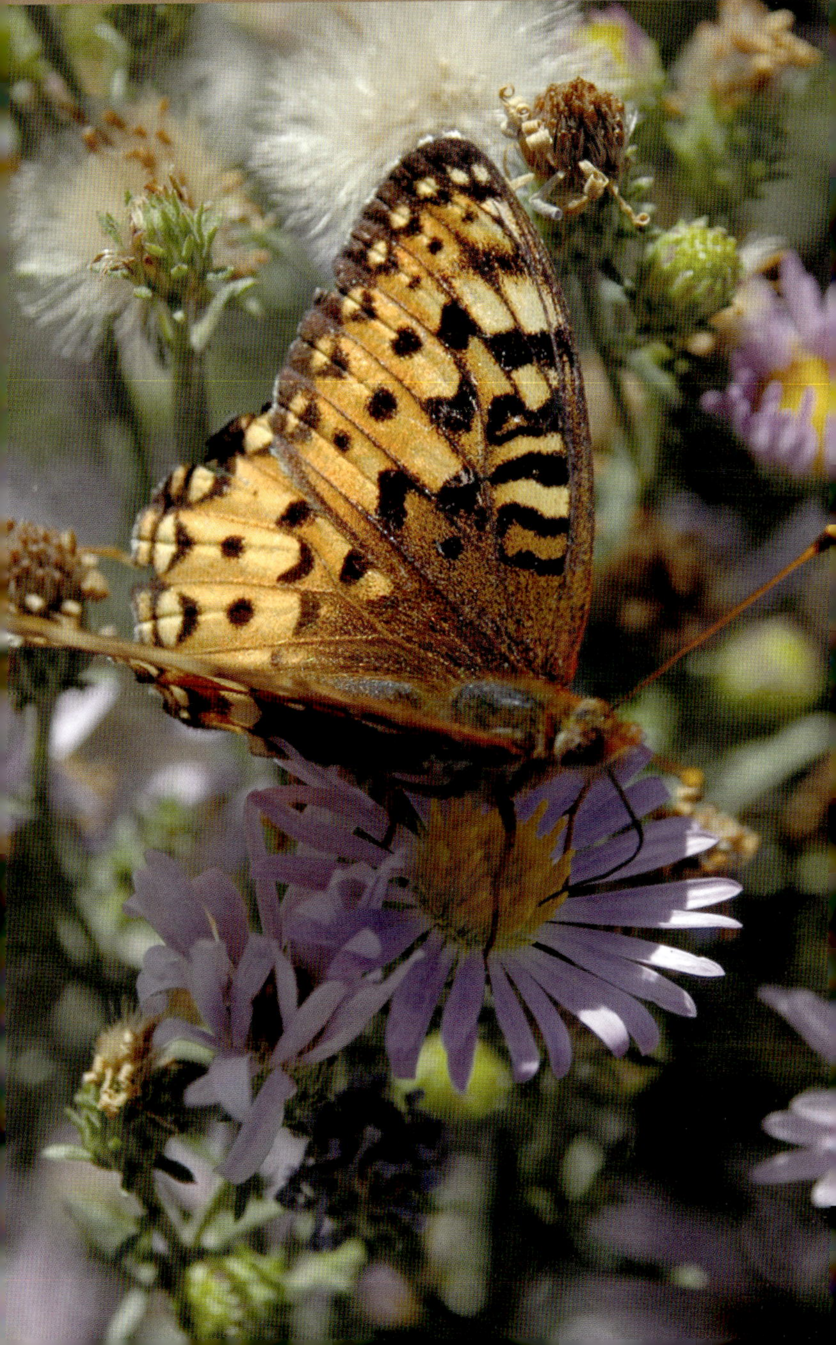

Great Basin Fritillary

Speyeria egleis

IDENTIFICATION: Wing span 1½ - 2⅜ inches. Upperside; orange-brown, marginal and submarinal spots paler, darker scaling in basal area. Underside; pale buff tone except brown disk, submarginal band includes brown caps on marginal spots, without orange flush on forewing base or small black spot above hindwing discal cell. Spots both silvered and unsilvered. Similar to Northwestern (more orange), Mormon (more green), Coronis (lacks caps on marginal spots), and Zerene frits (distinct black line on submarginal spots). Very difficult to distinguish and authors disagree on markings.

LIFE STAGES: Eggs laid near host plant, violets. Caterpillar will overwinter. Caterpillar is gray-brown with black and yellow bands and branching yellow-white spines. Flight June - August.

HABITAT: Pine, spruce and aspen forest, forest openings and meadows, watercourses.

(right) Great Spangled Fritillary underside

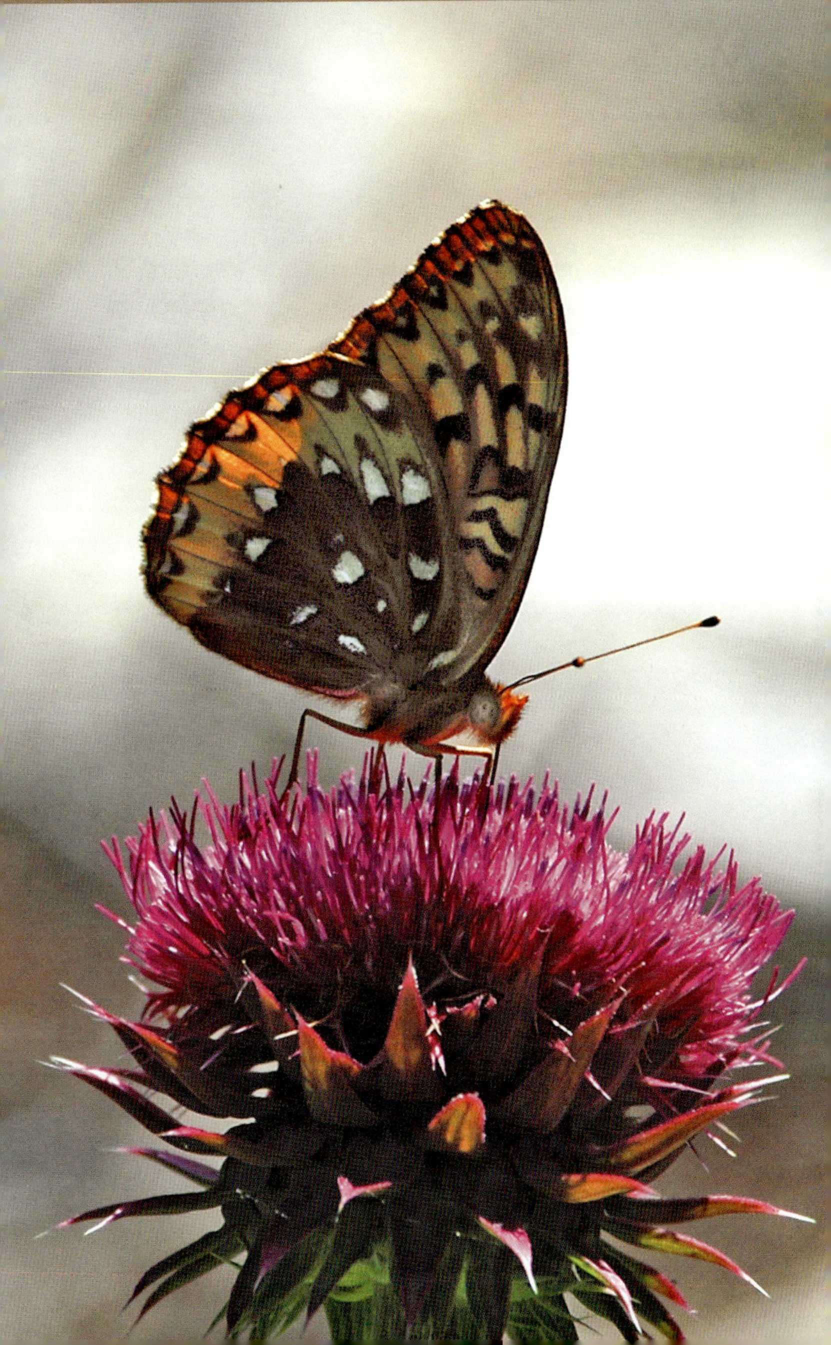

Meadow Fritillary

Boloria bellona

IDENTIFICATION: Wing span 1¼ - 1⅞. Forewing tip clipped. Upperside orange-brown with black markings, no dark marginal border. Underside; hindwing's white keel shaped patch on leading edge, marginal purplish row of spots and violet-gray background on outer half of wing. Similar Frigga Fritillary lacks forewing clip.

LIFE STAGES: Egg laid on plants near host violets. Caterpillar purple-black with yellow and black marking, brown spines. Caterpillar overwinters. Adults nectar at flowers, fly low in zig-zag. Flight June - July.

HABITAT: Moist meadows in forest openings. aspen meadows, willow bogs, and watercourses.

Frigga Fritillary

Boloria frigga

IDENTIFICATION: Wing span 1¼ - 1⅜ inches. Upperside; similar to other lesser fritillaries but with considerable dark scaling on basal half. Underside; forewing yellow patch with submarginal row of white centered black crescents, red scaling on margin and apex areas. Hindwing has a white patch at leading edge a darker basal area banded at median golden yellow and a violet-pink outer half.

LIFE STAGES: Caterpillar black body and spines with purple stripe on sides. Host plant willows. Chrysalis overwinters. Flight June – July.

HABITAT: Watercourse's and bogs with willows, alpine tundra.

Relict Fritillary

Boloria kriemhild

IDENTIFICATION: Wing span $1\frac{3}{8}$ - $1\frac{3}{4}$ inches. Fringes checkered. Upperside, bright orange-brown with black pattern, veins, and spots, submarginal chevrons pointing outward on forewing. Underside; forewing darker red-orange at base fading to yellow-orange on outer wing, chevrons point outward, hindwing red-orange with median cream checkered row outlined in black and black spots with light centers. Hindwing may have purplish scaling.

LIFE STAGES: Not documented. Host plant violets. Caterpillar hibernates. Adults nectar at flowers. Flight May thru July.

HABITAT: Alpine meadows, forest openings, and willow bottoms. Restricted to a small range in western Wyoming, parts of Montana, Idaho, and Utah.

(right) Submarginal chevrons point outward

Freija Fritillary

Boloria freija

IDENTIFICATION: Wing span 1¼ - 1½ inches. Upperside; tawny orange with black bars and spots, may have dark basal scaling. Underside; cream to yellow with reddish-brown markings, hindwing with white postmedian scalloped line and distinct white arrow shaped mark in center of wing.

LIFE STAGES: Tan egg laid near host bearberry or huckleberry. Caterpillar brown with lighter patches and many branching spines. Earliest fritillary to hatch in May – June.

HABITAT: Forest clearings, willow bogs, and alpine tundra.

Bog Fritillary

Boloria eunomia

IDENTIFICATION: Wing span 1¼ - 1⅝ inches. Upperside black markings on orange, darker in basal area. Underside; hindwing alternating cream-white to silver with orange bands, identifing mark is row of white spots outlined in black. Similar to Silver-Bordered Fritillary, which has black spots on hindwing below.

LIFE STAGES: 2 - 4 eggs laid on host leaves. Caterpillar gray-black with small white dots and white spines. Host plants reported violets and willows, perhaps bistort or blueberries. Flight mid June to August.

HABITAT: Bogs, damp alpine meadows. Local population found on beartooth pass.

Arctic Fritillary

Boloria chariclea

IDENTIFICATION: Wing span 1 $\frac{3}{16}$ - 1$\frac{1}{2}$ inches. Variable. Upperside; orange with black markings. Underside hindwing marginal white spots capped with brown, lighter median band center spot elongated, faint submarginal spots. Similar to Freja Fritillary which has black median line and Relict Fritillary which has inward pointing submarginal chevrons.

LIFE STAGES: Eggs laid on host. Caterpillar gray with black stripe and orange spines. Various hosts reported, blueberrys, bistort, violets, and willows. Flight June - July. May be biennial.

HABITAT: Damp watercourses, moist alpine meadows or bogs, may be at higher elevations.

(left) Photographed in Hanging Canyon, GTNP

Silver-Bordered Fritillary

Boloria selene

IDENTIFICATION: Wing span $1\frac{3}{8}$ - 2 inches. Upperside orange with black pattern of spots and bars. Underside, distinctinve silvered spots in medial and marginal rows, black submarginal spots. One black spot on basal hindwing. Similar to Bog Fritillary which has black ringed white underside submarginal spots, no silvering.

LIFE STAGES: Single egg laid near host plant. Caterpillar varies greenish to gray-black with yellow spines and mottling. Front thoracic pair of spines black. Caterpillar hibernates. Host plant violets. Adults are fast fliers, nectaring at yellow composites. Flight June - August.

HABITAT: Prefers wet areas near watercourses, marshes or alpine lakes.

Variegated Fritillary

Euptoieta claudia

IDENTIFICATION: Wingspan 1¾ - 2½ inches (up to 3¼ inches in some documentation). Outer forewing margin concave. Upperside; orange-brown with black markings darker at base, median band lighter tone, submarginal black spots on both wings. Underside; forewing similar to upper only lighter, hindwing with light veins and mottled markings brown, yellow, and orange, lighter marginal band without silvering. No similar species in this area.

LIFE STAGES: Single, cream colored, ribbed egg laid on host. Caterpillar orange-red with stripes of black and white patches on sides, also 6 rows of black spines and two longer spines on head. Caterpillar will eat a large variety of plants, notably violets, flax, and stonecrop. Migrant to area in June - August.

HABITAT: Sunny open areas, meadows, roadsides, sage, and grasslands.

Field Crescent

Phyciodes pratensis

IDENTIFICATION: Wing span 1 - 1½ inches. Antennal knob ends brown. Upperside is dark with orange and cream marks. Submarginal band orange with black spots in hindwing orange. Cream median band on forewing. Underside is orange-brown with yellow discal bar and small black patches on forewing inner margin. Hindwing patterned with yellow brown rusty markings.

LIFE STAGES: Eggs laid on underside of host leaves in large batches. Caterpillar is brown-black with tiny white dots, faint dorsal stripes and black head. Caterpillars hibernate. Host plants, asters and fleabanes. Adults patrol low to vegetation and sip flower nectar. Flight June - August.

HABITAT: Open areas, mountain glades, streamcourses, and marshes.

Pale crescent at center hindwing margin

FIELD CRESCENT   117

Mylitta Crescent

Phyciodes mylitta

IDENTIFICATION: Wing span 1 - 1½ inches. Outer margin of forewing is angled. Orange antennal knobs. Upperside bright red-orange with narrow black markings and black spots submarginally on hindwing. Underside orange-brown forewing with rusty markings. Hindwing with lighter patches, black submarginal spots, and white crescent.

LIFE STAGES: Eggs laid on underside of host leaves. Caterpillars black to maroon with white dots and paired white lines on sides and back. Spines on sides black or orange. Caterpillar may make silken nest. Host plants in thistle family. Adults patrol and sip nectar from a wide variety of flowers. Flight, two broods, April - September.

HABITAT: Open meadows and fields, streamcourses.

White crescent in hindwing margin

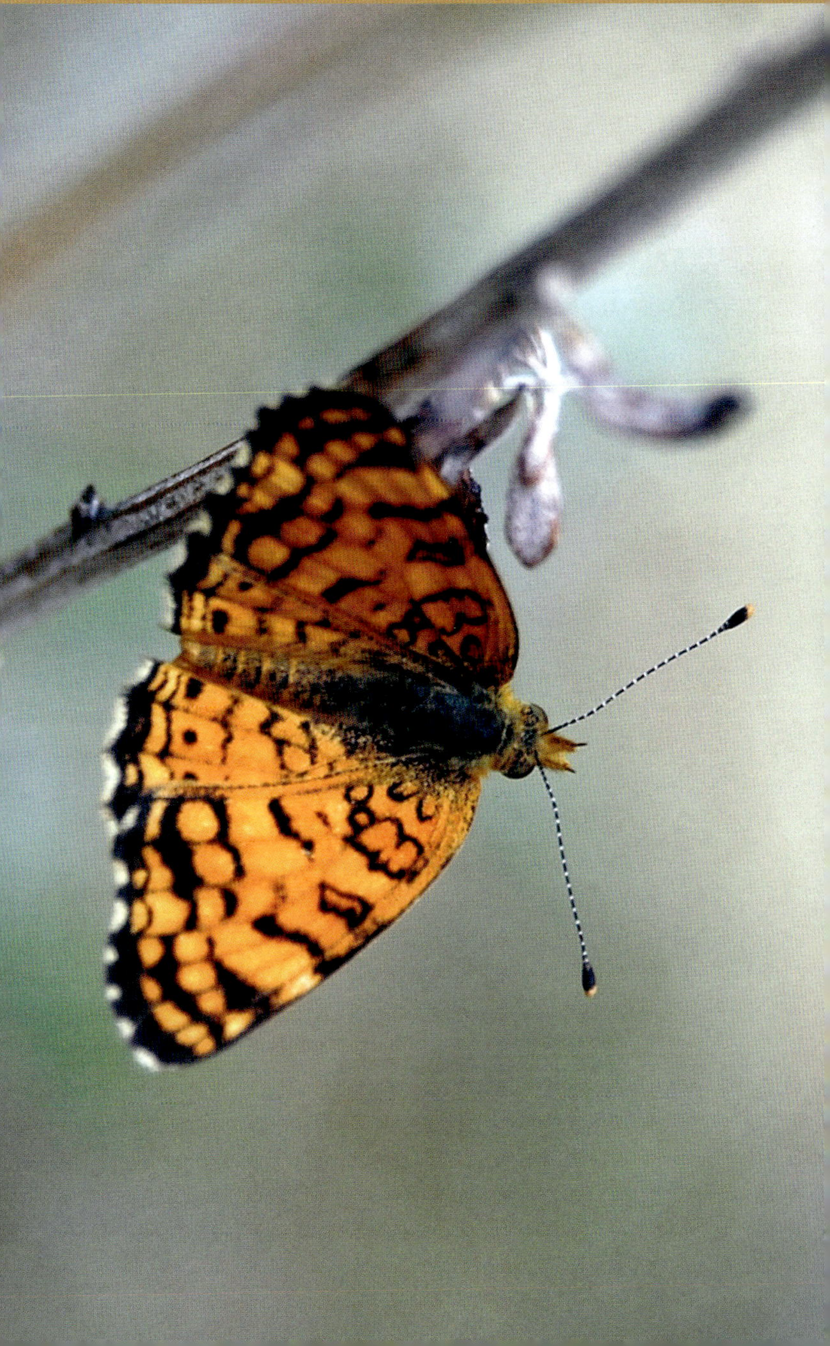

Pale Crescent

Phyciodes pallida

IDENTIFICATION: Wing span 1¼ - 1¾ inches. Upperside; pale orange with irregular black mark and spots, narrow black borders. Prominent black patch on rear margin of the forewing above and below. Underside; orange-yellow with rusty markings, lighter crescent in center of hindwing margin border. Similar to Mylitta Crescent which is smaller and darker.

LIFE STAGES: Eggs, cream color and ribbed, laid in clusters on the underside of host leaves. Caterpillar ocher with brown bands and branching spines, head black. Host plant thistles. Flight late May - June.

HABITAT: Gullies and watercourses in canyons, sage flats, also forest roadcuts and openings.

(right) Note the fly on apex

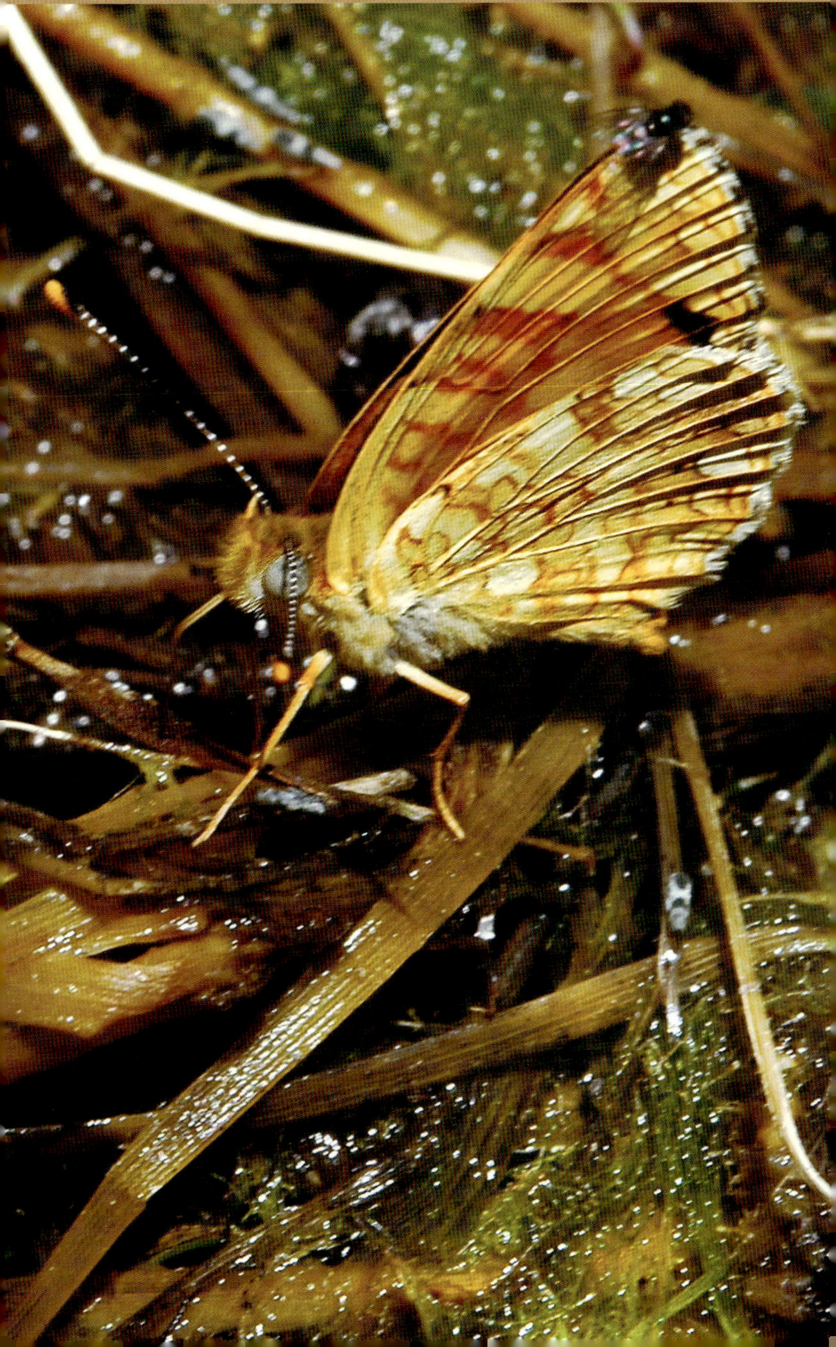

Northern Crescent

Phyciodes cocyta

IDENTIFICATION: Wing span 1¼ - 1⅞ inches. Orange tip on antennal club on males. Upperside has large orange-brown postmedian and submarginal area. Margins of both wings with wide black band, black spots on hindwing above black band. Jagged black lines on basal areas of both wings. Underside, hindwing has pale tan marginal crescent patch and pale jagged orange markings. Forewing with black patches on leading margin. Similar species, Pearl and Tawny Cresents, not found in our area.

LIFE STAGES: Eggs laid in bunches of 30 - 40 on underside of host plant leaves. Young caterpillars live communally, late brood will hibernate. Caterpillar is pinkish in color with spines grayer in tone than body. Host plant asters, adults sip nectar. Flight June - July.

HABITAT: Aspen groves. meadows. moist open areas near streams and marshes.

NORTHERN CRESCENT

Edith's Checkerspot

Euphydryas editha

IDENTIFICATION: Wing span 1 - 2 inches. Variable. Forewing rounded at tip. Abdomen black with red rings. Upperside is black with red and white bands and checkers. Submarginal band of white spots and postmedian red band broken by black veins. Underside of forewing has postmedian cream spots at lower edge. Hindwing postmedian red band extends into median cream band. Similar to Variable Checkerspot, which is larger and more pointed forewing.

LIFE STAGES: Eggs laid in groups on underside of flowers and leaves of host plants. Caterpillar black with white or orange spots or stripes and black spines. Caterpillars live in loose silk webs and eat leaves and flowers. Caterpillars hibernate. Host plants include paintbrush, honeysuckles, beardstongues, and lousewort. Adults sip nectar. Flight from Late May - August at our elevation.

HABITAT: Diverse areas, grassland, sagebrush, meadows, alpine tundra, and open woods.

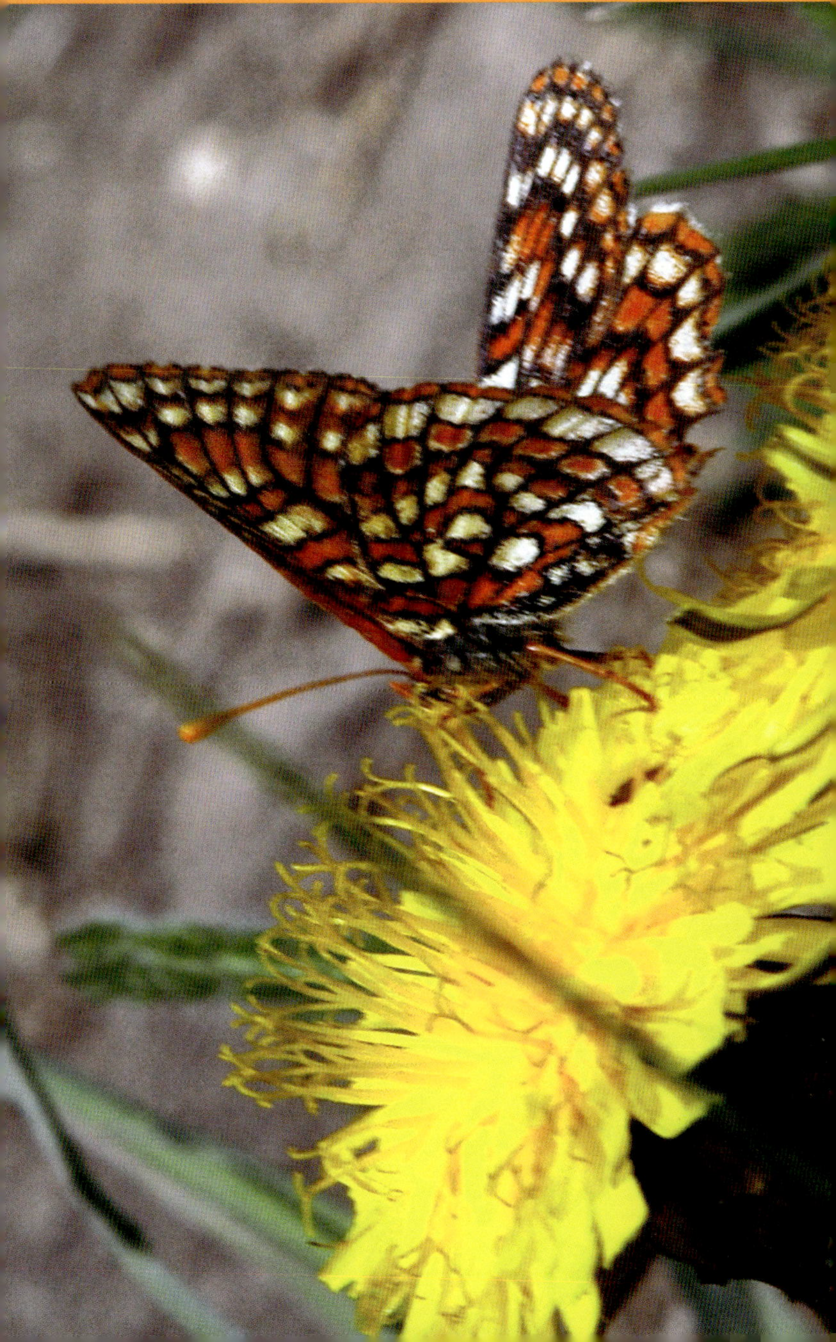

Variable Checkerspot

Euphydryas chalcedona

IDENTIFICATION: Wing span 1⅛ - 2¼ inches. Variable, many sub-species in complex assembly of populations that interbreed. Pictured are Chalcedon (black) and Anicia (red). Abdomen may have white dots

on sides. Forewing narrow. Upperside; black, banded red-orange and white or yellow. Underside; forewing orange with cream submarginal band(s). Hindwing alternating orange and cream bands, orange at margin. Similar species, Edith's checkerspot, lacks white abdomen spots and has rounded forewing.

LIFE STAGES: Eggs laid in large cluster on underside of leaves. Caterpillar variable, black or white with orange or black bristly tubercles. Overwinter in curled leaf of host. Hosts, paintbrush, monkey flower, penstemons, honey-suckles, and others. Flight May - August.

HABITAT: Forest openings, roadcuts, watercourses, scree slopes, and sagebrush flats.

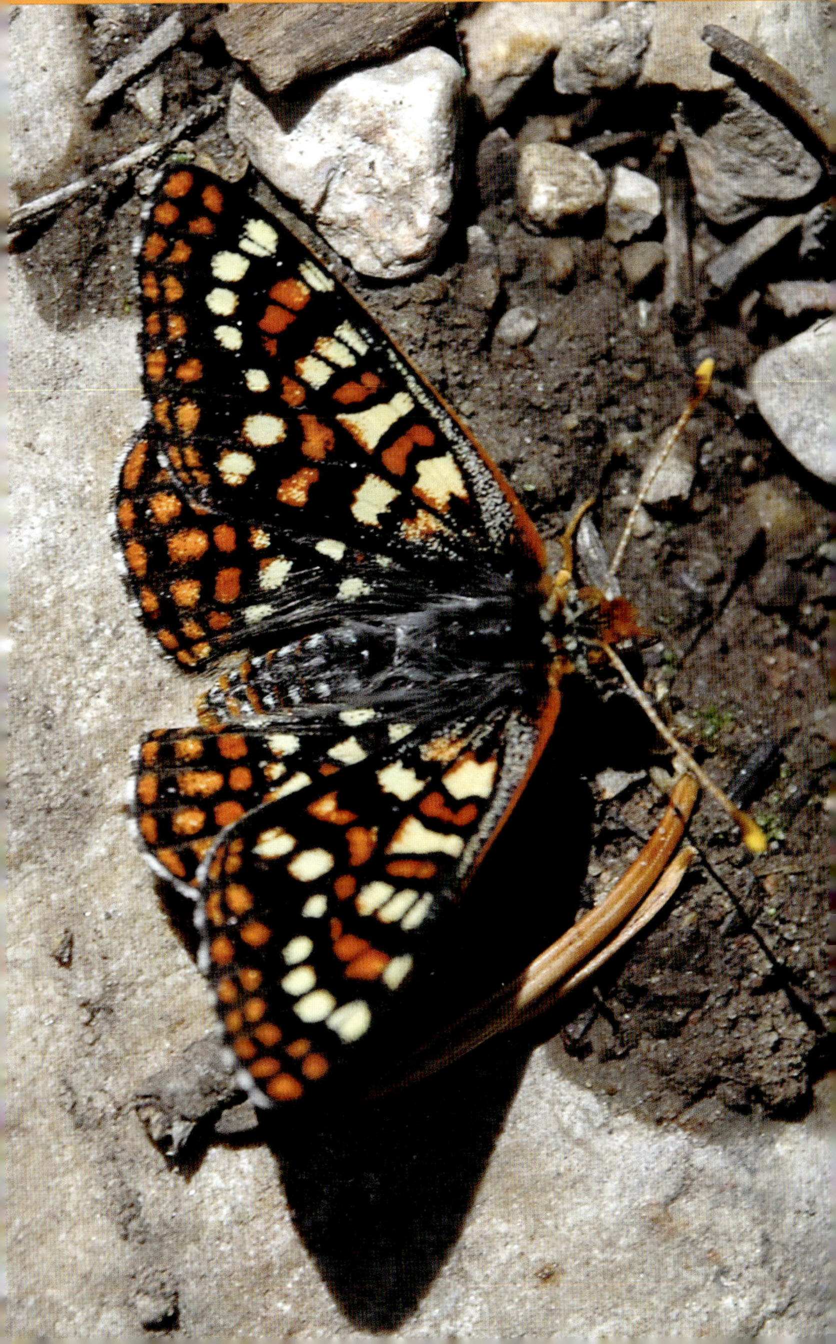

Gillette's Checkerspot, Yellowstone Checkerspot

Euphydryas gillettii

IDENTIFICATION: Wing span 1½ - 1¾ inches. Distinct appearance from other checkerspots. Upperside. wings black with a broad sub-marginal red orange band on both wings. Forewing has a orange red band proximal to margin, one red orange spot near margin, other spots white. Underside similar red orange bands and spots but other bands more white in appearance than upperside. No similar species.

LIFE STAGES: Eggs laid on underside of leaves in sun for additional warmth. Caterpillars live together in silk tents, are dark yellow with a yellow dorsal stripe and white lateral stripes. spines are yellow on top and black on sides. Host plant usually bearberry honeysuckle in our area. Caterpillar may overwinter two years at this elevation. Adults are weak fliers and nectar at flowers. Flight June - August.

HABITAT: Forest openings near moist meadows and streamcourses.

Sagebrush Checkerspot

Chlosyne acastus

IDENTIFICATION: Wing span 1¼ - 1¾ inches. Upperside; checkered brownish-orange to yellow orange, black lines variable in width. Underside; mottled orange on forewing, hindwing, black rimmed, cream colored banding and crescents, alternating with narrow orange areas. Very similar to Northern Checkerspot which is usually brighter colored and yellowish rather than cream or white below.

LIFE STAGES: Eggs laid on underside of host leaf in clusters. Caterpillar black, very spiny, with orange crescents and white dots. Caterpillar hibernates. Host plants asters and rabbitbrush. Adults bask in hot sunny areas with wings open.

HABITAT: Arid sagebrush and grasslands near forest edges.

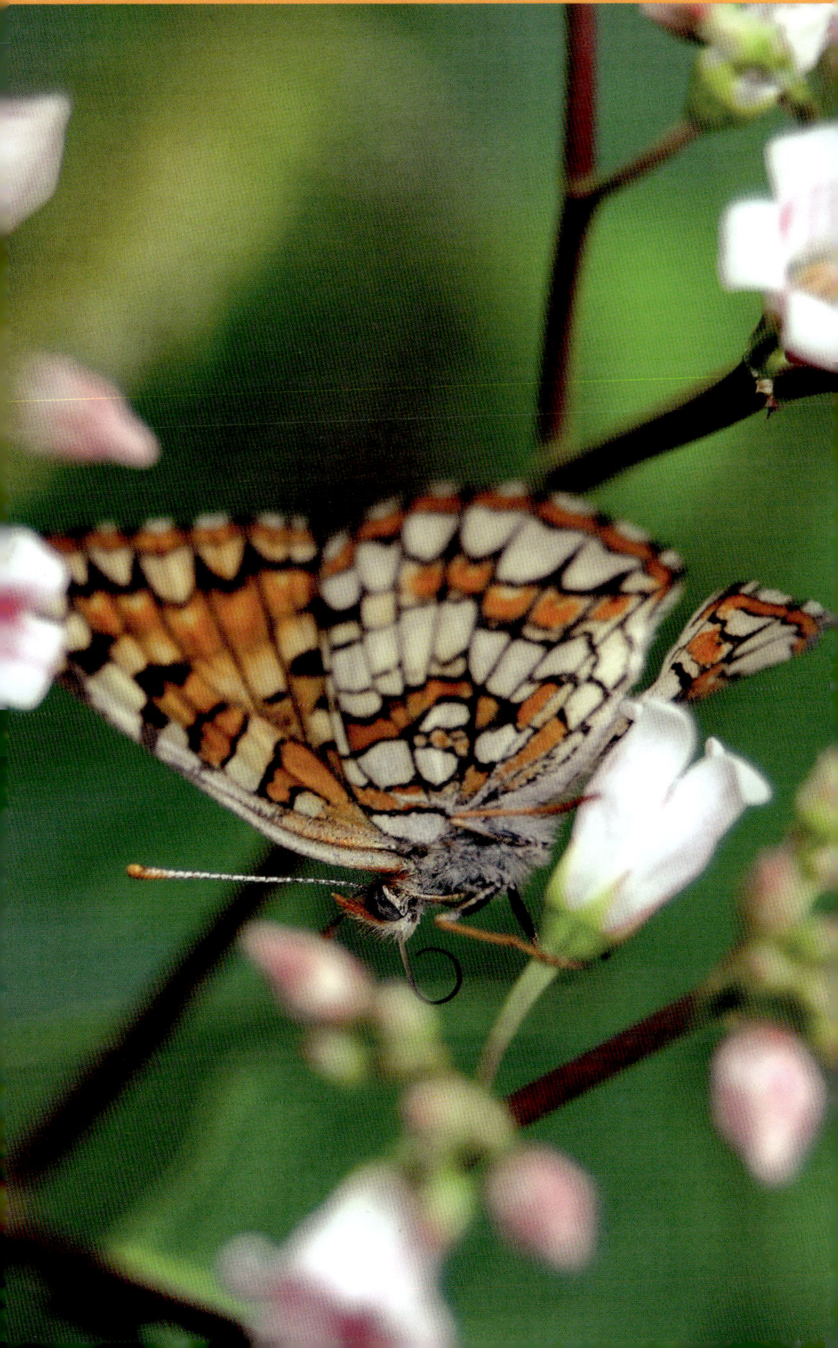

Northern Checkerspot

Chlosyne palla

IDENTIFICATION: Wing span 1⅜ - 1¾ inches. Black and white fringes. Upperside; males orange-brown, may be redder in forewing cell and marginal band. Hindwing base darker. Females similar or may be more black with white-yellow pattern. Underside, alternating rows of cream-yellow and red-orange checkers on hindwing, forewing mostly orange with cream submarginal row and black checks on forewing margin. Similar to Sagebrush and Rockslide Checkerspots, location may be only way to differentiate these closely related species.

LIFE STAGES: Eggs laid in groups on underside of leaves. Caterpillar black with white dots and orange dashes on sides and very spiny. Host plants rabbitbrush, asters. fleabane, goldenrod, and indian paintbrush. Flight May -July.

HABITAT: Watercourses, meadows, sagebrush, and forest openings.

Rockslide Checkerspot

Chlosyne whitneyi

IDENTIFICATION: Wing span 1¼ - 1½ inches. Upperside; checkered bands of orange-red, sometimes brown, with glossy black lines. Underside; forewing orange with black lines with a cream submarginal band and orange margin. Hindwing cream with irregular orange median band and black lines. Similar species Northern and Sagebrush checkerspots usually not found at high elevations.

LIFE STAGES: Eggs laid in clusters on underside of leaves. Young caterpillar will overwinter, sometimes two years. Caterpillar black with spines and orange stripes and cream dots. Host plants in composite family, fleabane, goldenrod, and alpine sunflower. Flight July - August.

HABITAT: Rocky alpine slopes, trails or roads, above treeline.

Green Comma

Polygonia faunus

IDENTIFICATION: Wing span 1½ - 2 inches. Exceptionally ragged wing edges. Upperside; red-brown with wide dark border with light spots, forewing inner two spots usually fused, three separate black spots below, edge narrowly gray. Hindwing has submarginal white-yellow spots. Underside; brown to gray, submarginal green spots, silver spot L or C shaped. Similar to Hoary Comma.

LIFE STAGES: Eggs, pale green, laid singly on upper side of host leaves. Caterpillar yellow-brown to red with white back and spines, orange lateral bands with transverse black and yellow spots, head black with a white W marking. Caterpillars eat host plants, pussy willow, aspens, birch, alder and gooseberry. Adults emerge mid to late summer and hibernate to mate in the spring. Adult prefer sap and dung to flower nectar.

HABITAT: Openings in forest, roadcuts and steamsides.

Overwintering adult

Sipping on photographer's glove

GREEN COMMA

Satyr Comma

Polygonia satyrus

IDENTIFICATION: Wing span 1½ - 2 1/16 inches. Upperside is bright yellow orange, forewing with two black spots on trailing edge and black border on outer margin. Hindwing lacks the well defined dark border and has a black spot in center of wing. Underside is mottled golden brown, the median band is relatively straight with comma, clubbed and bent at top, in the center.

LIFE STAGES: Eggs laid in stacks or singly in groups on the underside of nettle leaves. Caterpillars eat leaves and live in folded leaf shelter fastened with silk. Caterpillar is banded green-white with lateral spines black, dorsal spines green-white. Adults sip nectar and tree sap. Flight in April - September. Adults overwinter.

HABITAT: Along streams and marshes and in openings near moist areas of conifer forest.

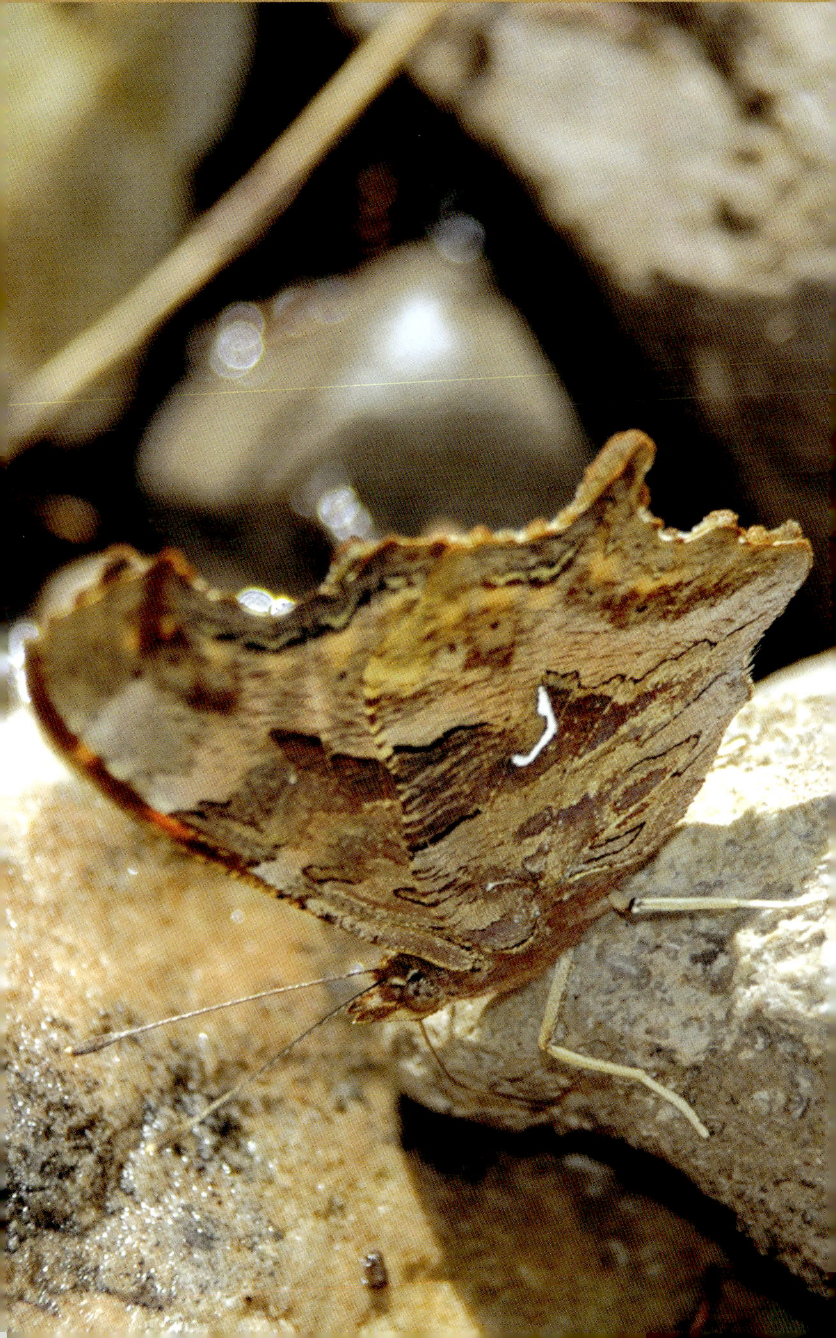

Hoary Comma

Polygonia gracilis

IDENTIFICATION: Wing span 1½ - 2¼ inches. Upperside red-orange with darker borders, hindwing with yellowish submarginal spots. Underside is gray-brown the outer half is distinctly lighter "hoary" white or silver. Fishhook spot, tapered at both ends, in center of hingwing. Similar to Green Comma, with 2 costal spots fused.

LIFE STAGES: Eggs laid on underside of host leaves. Caterpillar is black-brown, with spines, front half reddish streaks, upper part of rear abdomen white. Host plants, currents, gooseberry and menziesia. Adults sip flower nectar, overwinter and lay eggs until June with the flight from July - September.

HABITAT: Woodlands near streams and openings, brushlands. Wanders to many habitats.

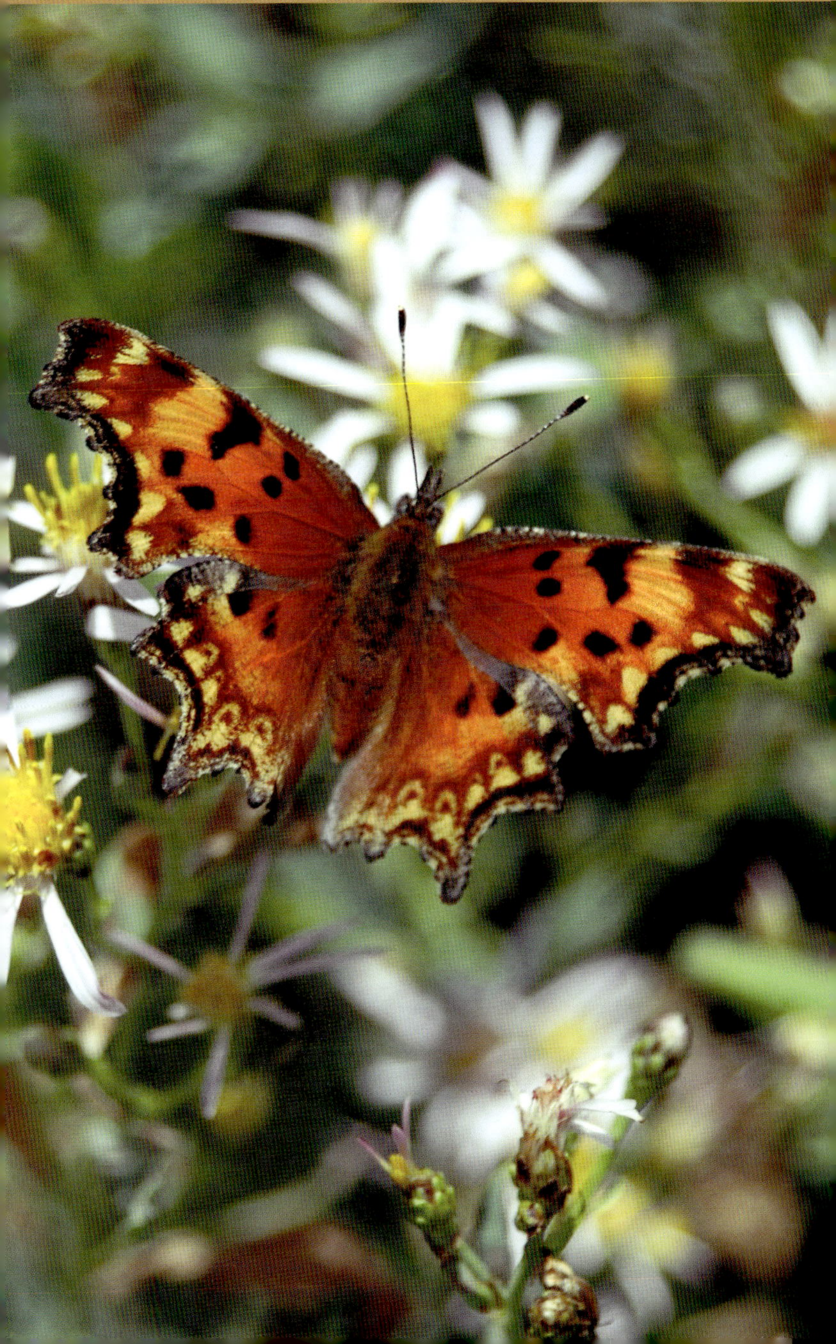

Gray Comma

Polygonia progne

IDENTIFICATION: Wing span 1¾ - 2 inches. Upperside; orange-brown with dark border and small spots on forewing, hindwing has wide dark border with yellow submarginal spots in border. Underside; gray-brown, without much contrast between inner and outer halves, comma L shaped and tapered at ends. Similar to Oreas and Hoary commas. Oreas Comma (*Polygonia oreas*), which may be in this area, has larger blended dark spots and bigger pale spots in wing margin on upperside and underside is like gray comma but darker brown.

LIFE STAGES: Single, green ribbed, egg laid on host currant (*Ribes*) or gooseberry. Caterpillar variable colors with darker V shaped marks and spines, dark head with W marking and two black spines. Adults, overwinter, prefer sap to nectar and are reported to be slow fliers. Spring and fall flights.

HABITAT: Aspen forest and forest openings such as trails, roads, and clearings.

Compton Tortoiseshell

Nymphalis vaualbum

IDENTIFICATION: Wing span 2½ - 3 inches. Larger than other anglewings. Upperside; forewing yellow orange with large black spots and a white spot on leading edge. hindwing single black spot edged outwardly by white. Underside mottled gray brown, inner half darker with single V shaped white mark like commas. Similar to California Tortoiseshell which lacks white hindwing spots on upper and under hindwing. Underside may be confused with other anglewings.

LIFE STAGES: Cluster of eggs laid on host. Caterpillar green with speckles and black branching spines. Host plants aspen, willow and birch, perhaps poplar. Overwintering adults sip willow nectar, sap and dung. Species migates to this area from the north. Flight May - September.

HABITAT: Clearings in deciduous forest, watercourses.

Milbert's Tortoiseshell

Nymphalis milberti

IDENTIFICATION: Wing span 1½ - 2½ inches. Forewing tip squared off, irregular wing margins, two toned. Upperside basel portion is black with two costal orange spots. Outer half is orange grading to yellow at inner edge. Black margin border on both wings with blue spots in hindwing border. Similar species California Tortoiseshell is larger without black basal coloring. Underside like dead leaf with basal half much darker.

LIFE STAGES: Green eggs laid in large batches of hundreds on underside of the host, nettles leaves. Caterpillars are black with white flecks, a lateral yellow and green stripe and 7 rows of spines. Young caterpillars feed together from web, older ones feed alone and fold leaf shelter from silk. Adults feed on flowers and hibernate overwinter. One or possibly two flights usually June.

HABITAT: Moist areas near woodlands, streamsides, meadows, and springs. Local and altitudinal movements are not well understood.

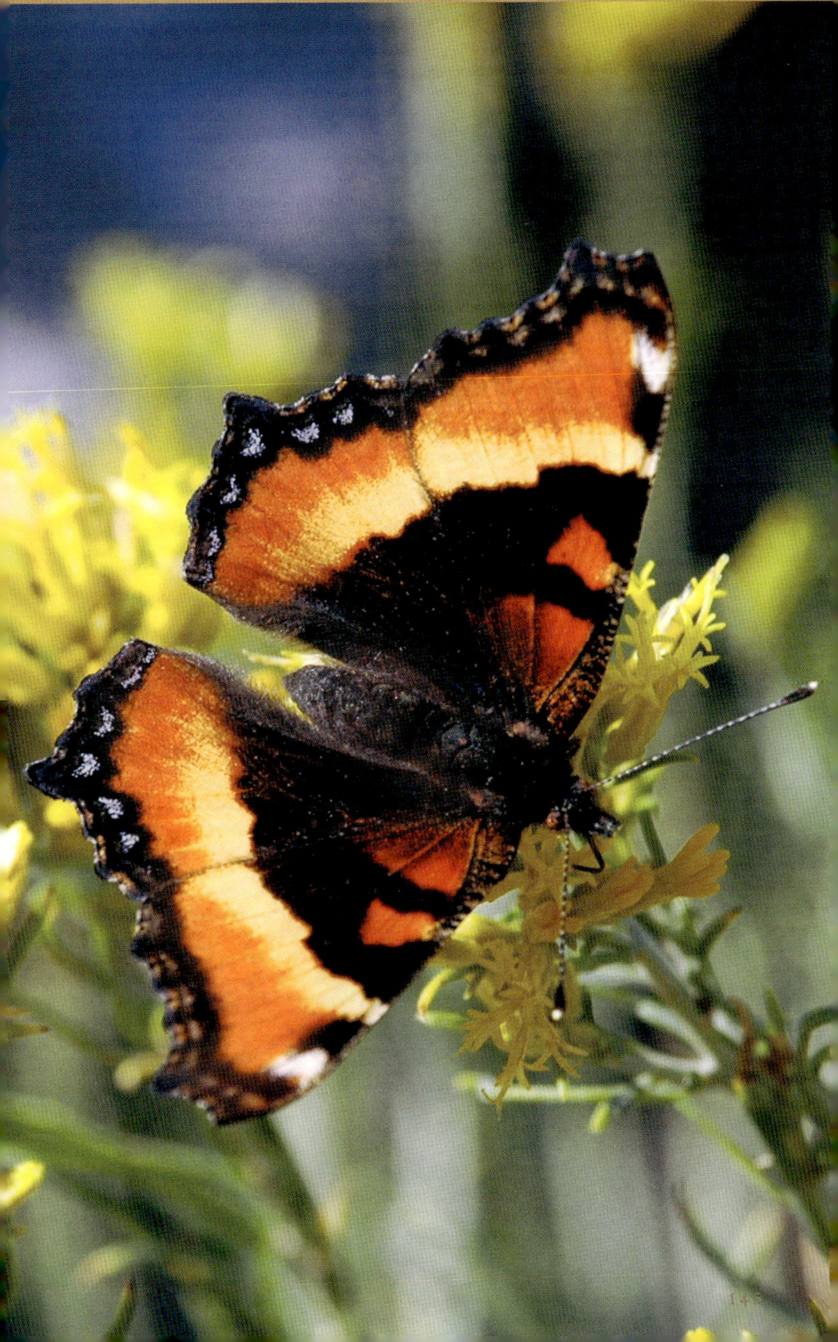

Mourning Cloak

Nymphalis antiopa

IDENTIFICATION: Wing span 2¼ - 4 inches. One of our most familiar butterflies, not easily confused with other species. Short projections on both wings and the margins are irregular. Upperside is brown to purplish brown with bright yellow border on both wings with a row of blue spots inside border.

LIFE STAGES: Eggs are laid in groups that may encircle the twig of the host plant. The caterpillar is black with white flecks, black spines, and red spots. They live together in a communal web and feed together on leaves. Caterpillars feed on willows, American elm, cottonwood, aspen, paper birch, and hackberry. Mourning Cloak adults prefer tree sap and rotting fruit, and only occasionally feed on flower nectar. The flight is in June - July but they are a long lived butterfly that may live 10-12 months, they can overwinter and be seen in the spring.

HABITAT: Mourning Cloaks roam and migrate so they are found in a wide variety of habitats but especially riparian areas.

Underside coloration

MOURNING CLOAK

California Tortoiseshell

Nymphalis californica

IDENTIFICATION: Wing span 1¾ - 2¾ inches. Upperside; orange with large black spots and small white spots on leading margin and dark wing borders. Underside; mottled dark brown, darkest at base, a lining of blue at margin. Similar to Milbert's Tortoiseshell.

LIFE STAGES: Eggs laid in bunches on host plant, ceanothus or snowbrush. Caterpillars eat leaves, feeding together when young. Caterpillars are black with white dots, yellow and bluish spines. Adults sip flower nectar and hibernate. Known to have periodic massive population outbreaks and emigrations in west.

HABITAT: Woodland, brushy areas, and forest edges. Migrates.

Note hummingbird feeder

White Admiral, Red Spotted Purple

Limenitis arthemis

IDENTIFICATION: Wing span 2⅝ – 3⅛ inches. Upperside; Black wings, iridescent purple-blue, with wide white post median band, hindwing with a submarginal series of red spots and marginal blue crescents. Underside; wing red-brown with white band repeated and red spots in basal areas and red submarginal band. Similar to much more common Weidemeyer's Admiral which lacks iridescent blues and red-brown on underside.

LIFE STAGES: Egg white and round. Late instar of caterpillar resembles bird dropping, shiny off white mottled gray-brown with a bristled hump behind head. Host plants willow and aspen, perhaps hawthorn in this area. Cream colored chrysalis. Adults prefer carrion, rotting fruit, and dung to flowers. Flight June – August. May hybridize with other Limenitis.

HABITAT: Roads and clearings in wooded areas, forest edges. This butterfly is a rare visitor to the area.

(right) Lorquin's Admiral may appear in area as migrant.

Weidemeyer's Admiral

Limenitis weidemeyerii

IDENTIFICATION: Wing span 2 - 2½ inches. Upperside is black with median white band on both wings. Submarginal area is black with small white spots on forewing and broken white margin on both wings. Underside is white with black veins and black submarginal stripes. Brown markings in black stipes at basal area of forewing and in submarginal stripe of hindwing. Similar to White Admiral which has blue reflections on upperside black.

LIFE STAGES: Eggs laid singly on tips of host leaves. Caterpillar is humpbacked, yellow-green with bristly spines on thorax. Host plants willows, aspen, cottonwood, chokecherry, and serviceberry. Flight June - September with one one two broods.

HABITAT: Forest, streamsides, aspen groves, and communities.

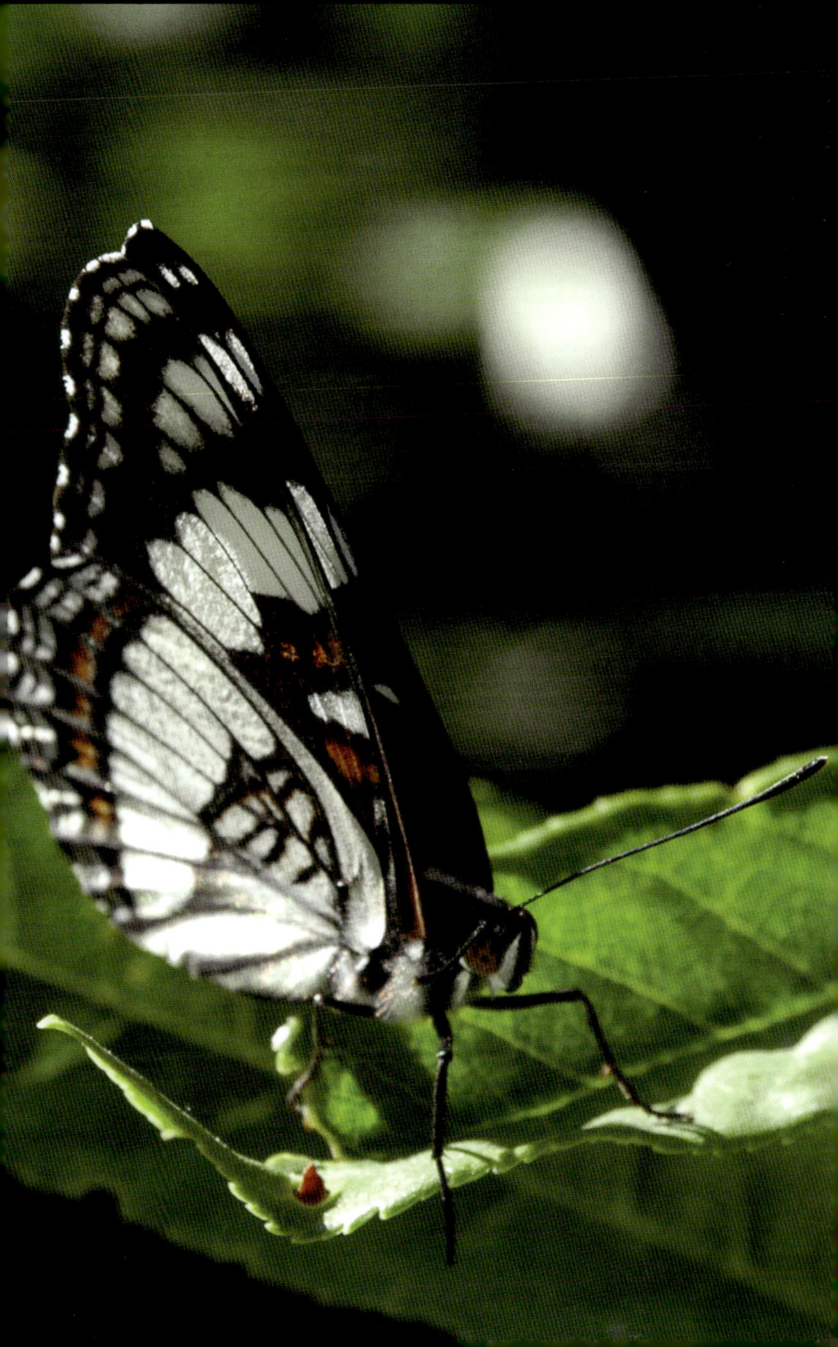

Painted Lady

Vanessa cardui

IDENTIFICATION: Wingspan 1¾ - 2½ inches. Upperside; orange brown, black apex with white bar and spots. Hindwing has black submarginal spots that may include blue scaling. Underside; forewing similar to upper but gray brown replaces the black. Hindwing mottled gray brown with four unequal eyespots. Similar to West Coast Lady with underside hindwing darker.

LIFE STAGES: Eggs laid singly on host plant. Variable caterpillar will make silk nest and eat leaves from a large variety of plants, but prefers thistles. Flight May thru August.

HABITAT: This butterfly is a colonist to our area as it cannot survive the freezing temperatures. Perhaps the most widespread butterfly in the world, it's found in open areas such as forest meadows, roadcuts, lakeshores, and ridgetops.

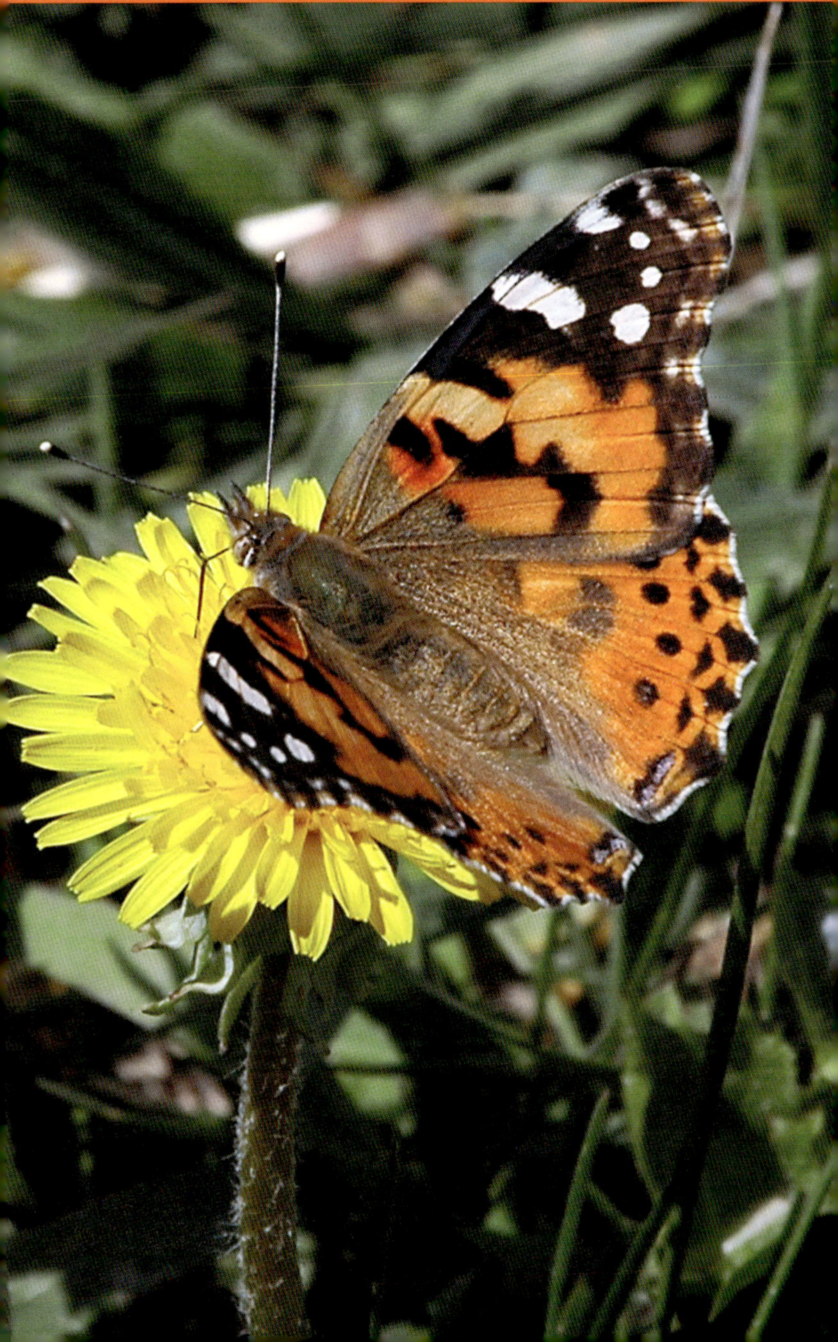

West Coast Lady

Vanessa annabella

IDENTIFICATION: Wing span 1¼ - 2 inches. Upperside; orange with black markings, apex black with white spots at tip and orange spot on leading margin. Hindwing with 3 - 4 blue submarginal spots. Underside; forewing base salmon color, buff colored costal bar and tip, white spots and markings, hindwing mottled buff, brown, tan with indistinct eyespots. Similar to American lady which has a white forewing costal bar and fewer blue spots on hindwing above.

LIFE STAGES: Green, barrel shaped, egg laid singly on host. Caterpillar is variable tan-black with spines and yellow-orange blotches, lines. Host mallows (Malvaceae), hollyhock, perhaps nettles. Migrant to our area, will not tolerate cold winters. Flight July - September.

HABITAT: Open canyons, meadows, roadcuts, and flowerbeds.

Red Admiral

Vanessa atalanta

IDENTIFICATION: Wing span $1\frac{3}{4}$ - $2\frac{1}{2}$ inches. Upperside wings black with white spots at apex and a red marginal band in forewing and red submarginal band in hindwing. Underside forewing with red marginal band and blue scaling on leading edge and above marginal band. White bar and spots in brown mottled apex. Hindwing mottled black brown with blue green scaling in submarginal spots.

LIFE STAGES: Eggs laid singly on host plant, nettles or perhaps hops. Caterpillar color variable black - green with yellow lateral stripes and branched spines. Caterpillars live in folded leaves. Adults have quick erratic flight and prefer tree sap and rotting fruit to flower nectars. Flight April thru September.

HABITAT: This butterfly is a migrant to this area as it cannot survive the cold winters. Found in openings near moist areas such as streamcourses and marshes. Males will perch on ridgetops. Will migrate through many habitats.

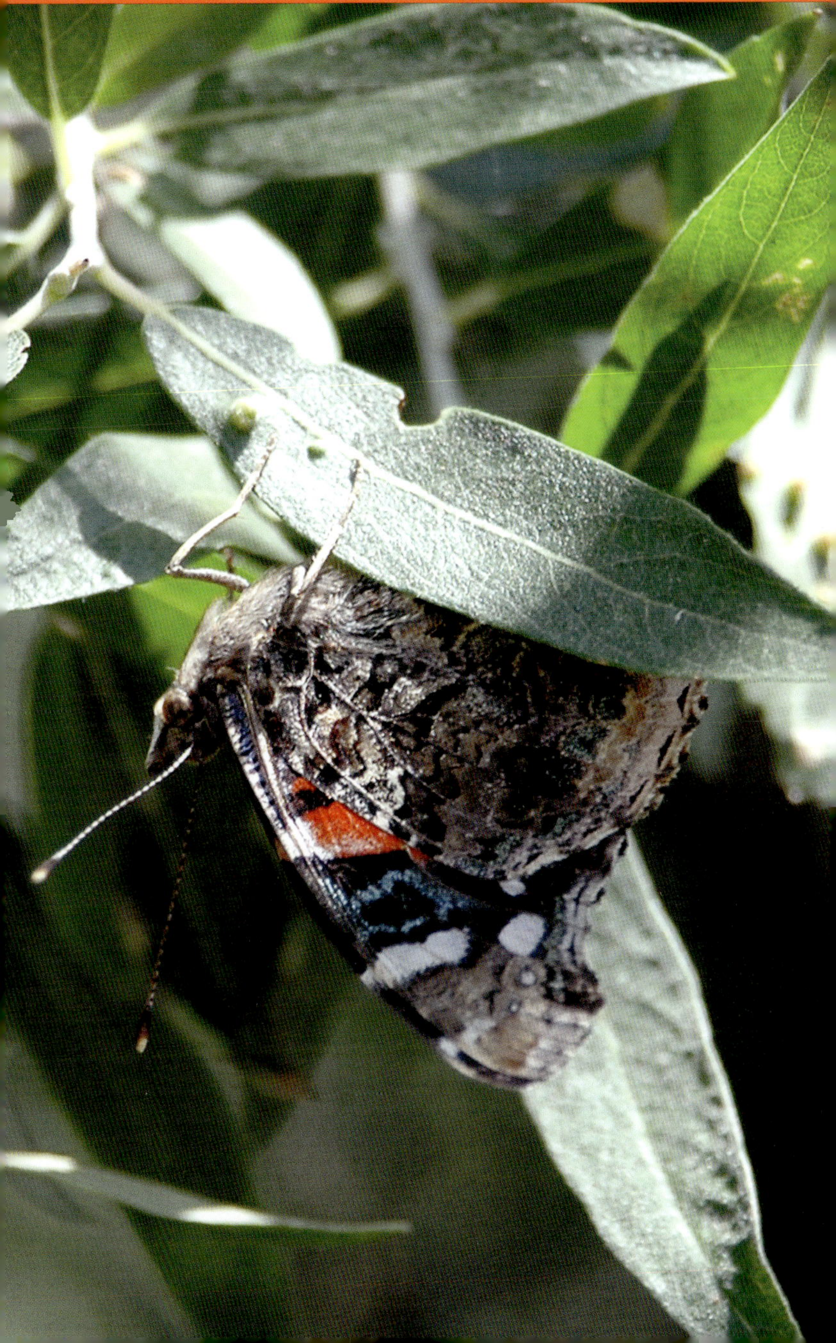

Viceroy

Limenitis archippus

IDENTIFICATION: Wing span 2¼ - 3 inches. Upperside and lowerside similar. Orange with black veins and margins, single row of white spots in margin and in black band cutting forewing tip. Single black line crossing hindwing is the variation from similar species Monarch.

LIFE STAGES: Two or three eggs laid at tip of leaf. Caterpillar humpbacked, mottled olive-brown with white dorsal saddle patch and two black bristles on thorax. Host plants willow, poplar, and cottonwood. Adults sip flower nectar. Flight May - September.

HABITAT: Prefers open wet areas, forest watercourses, lake edges, and swamps.

REMARKS: This butterfly is a mimic of the Monarch, but is probably not palatable to birds in its own right.

Black line crossing hindwing

Monarch

Danaus plexippus

IDENTIFICATION: Wing span 3 - 4½ inches. This is perhaps the most familiar butterfly. Upperside of male is bright orange with a black scent patch in middle of hindwing. Female is duller orange. Both with black veins and black border containing two rows of white spots. Underside is similar coloring. The head and upper thorax are black with white spots.

LIFE STAGES: Eggs laid singly on underside of milkweed leaves. The caterpillars eat the leaves and flowers. Caterpillar is transversely ringed with yellow, black and white on each segment with three pairs of fleshy black spines on back. The head is black and white striped. Adults sip necter from the milkweed flower and visit many other flowers during the early and late seasons. Early flowers include the dogbane, lilac, clover, and thistles, the late season is composites such as the goldenrods and blazing stars. Similar species found in parts of our area, the Viceroy, has a black median line crossing hindwing . The adults migrate annually, flying thousands of miles, to central Mexico and southern California. The massive winter roost sites in Mexico, with millions of butterflies, are important areas for conservation. The flight in northern America during spring and summer may be 1 - 3 broods in the north and 4 - 6 broods in the south.

HABITAT: Open areas, prairies, fields, meadows, weedy areas, pastures, marshes, and roadsides. Ranges from southern Canada throughout entire continental United States, Central America, and most of South America.

REMARKS: The adult Monarch stores cardiac glycosides, derived from the caterpillars milkweed hosts. These poisonous chemicals are both distasteful and emetic to predators who eat them. This chemical protection, in combination with the bright colors, may serve as a deterent to the predator eating Monarchs in the future.

MONARCH

Common Ringlet

Coenonympha tullia

IDENTIFICATION: Wing span 1 - 1½ inches. Highly variable geographically. Sometimes considered to be different subspecies. Upperside in Rocky Mountain region is yellow-cream to yellow-orange. Underside variable as upperside but frequently darker. The forewing often has a dark eyespot near the tip and may have faint median band. The hindwing is gray green and usually has an irregular wavy white median band that may be discontinuous. May also have a series of submarginal eyespots or pale spots. No similar species.

LIFE STAGES: Caterpillar found in grasses. The caterpillar is green or brown with pale stripes and short paired tails at rear. Caterpillars hibernate in mats of dead grass. Adults patrol low to grasses with a bouncy flight and sip flower nectar. Flights are widely variable by region, in our area mid May thru August.

HABITAT: Open grassy areas in a wide variety of habitats and biomes.

Hayden's Ringlet

Coenonympha haydenii

IDENTIFICATION: Wing span 1½ - 1¾ inches. Upperside male brown to dark brown, without markings, female lighter. Underside both wings with a narrow row of pale metallic scales and terminal line. Hindwing has submarginal row of black eyespots ringed with orange. Similar to Common Alpine which has larger eyespots on forewing in orange base.

LIFE STAGES: Single egg laid on host plant leaves. Caterpillar yellow-green with white stripes. Caterpillar will nest in curled leaves tied with silk. Host plant grasses. Adults have slow skipping flight. Adults sip flower nectar. Flight from Late May - August.

HABITAT: Mountain meadows, forest openings, marshes and bogs. Unique to greater Yellowstone area.

Great Basin Wood Nymph

Cercyonis sthenele

IDENTIFICATION: Wing span 1⅛ – 2 inches. Upperside; brown, with two forewing eye spots, yellow with black then a white pupil. Underside; forewing with two eye spots, equal distance from margin, upper spot is usually larger than lower spot, outer third of hindwing lighter than median or basal area. Hindwing postmedian line indented in same cell as the eyespot. Similar to the Small Wood Nymph which has different hindwing postmedian line marking. Common Wood Nymph has the forewing eyespot size reversed with larger one on the bottom.

LIFE STAGES: Single egg laid on stems, egg hibernates. Caterpillar light green with white stripes on back and white dashes on sides. Nectars at flowers. Host plant willows. Flight June - July.

HABITAT: Sagebrush flats, Juniper or open conifer woodland.

Small Wood Nymph

Cercyonis oetus

IDENTIFICATION: Wing span 1¼ - 1¾ inches. Wings variable brown tone. Upperside forewing with one eyespot and dark stigma patch on male, two eyespots on female. Underside forewing with two eyespots, lower spot smaller and displaced toward the wing margin. Hindwing usually without eyespots and the middle portion of the postmedian line shaped like two adjacent mountain peaks pointing outward. Similar to larger Great Basin Wood-Nymph.

LIFE STAGES: Females lay single egg on host grasses. Caterpillar hibernates unfed until the following spring. Caterpillar has green head, body is yellow to light green with white hairs and dark green-yellow stripe on back and sides. Adults sip nectar from flowers. Flight June - August.

HABITAT: Brushlands, sage and scrub meadow, foothills, and grassy meadows.

Dark stigma patch

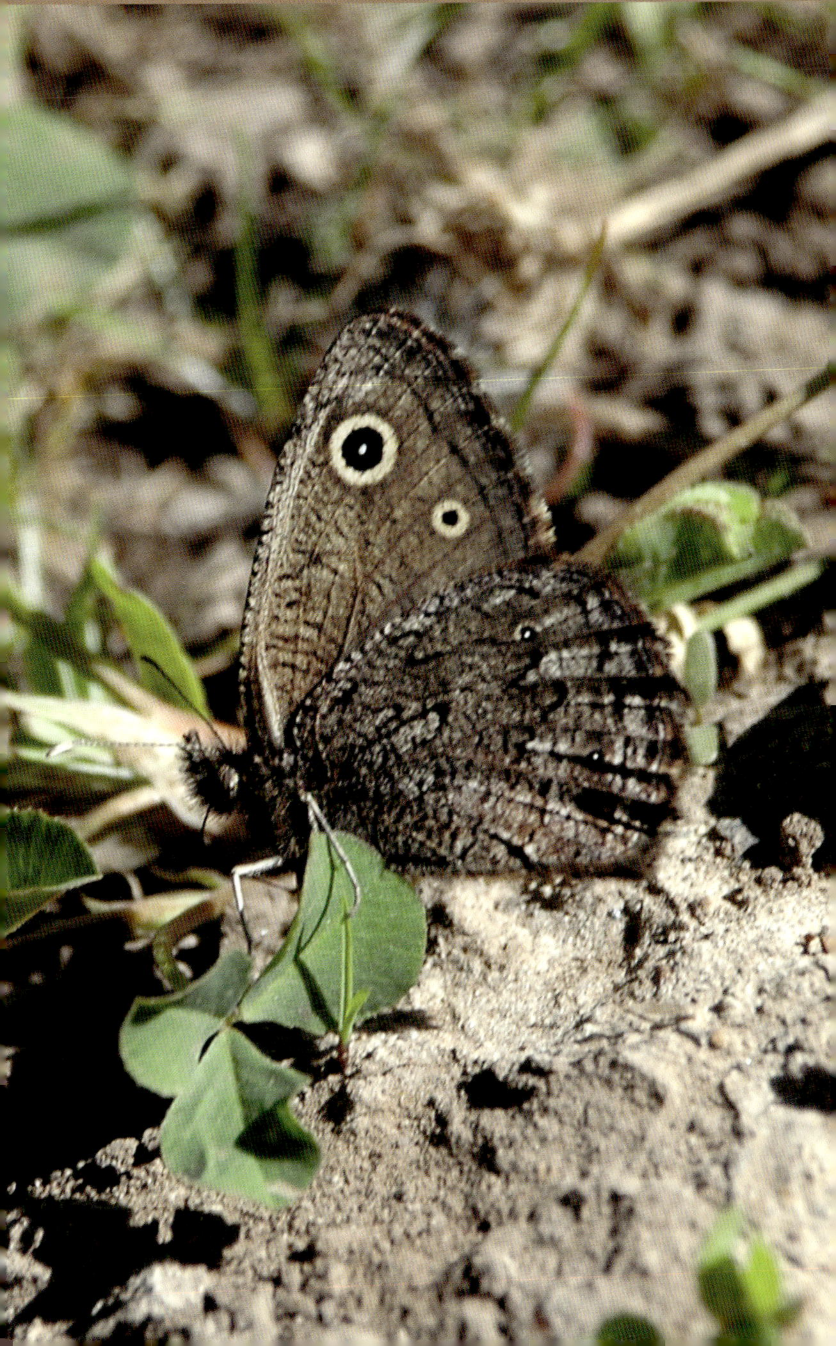

Common Wood Nymph

Cercyonis pegala

IDENTIFICATION: Wing span 1¾ - 2¾ inches. Geographically variable. Wings are brown. Sexes may differ in color and pattern. Upperside of forewing has two large yellow rimmed eyespots, but this may not be useful because wood-nymphs rarely open their wings when landed. Underside of forewing with two large yellow ringed black eyespots, the center may be blue rather than white. The bottom eyespot is larger than the top one, this is a good way to differentiate from the other Wood Nymphs. Hindwing with variable number of smaller eyespots. Striations on wings also quite variable. Flight late May - September. Two similar species of the Wood Nymph are found in this area. Great Basin Wood Nymph is smaller with underside forewing eyespot larger on top. The hindwing postmedian line is indented in the same cell as the largest HW eyespot. Small Wood Nymphs are smaller than others and have noticably smaller lower forewing eyespot that is displaced to the wing margin. The middle portion of the hindwing postmedian line is shaped like two adjacent mountain peaks. Mead's Wood Nymph, is not documented in this area but can be found nearby in eastern Wyoming, Montana, Colorado, and Utah, has a reddish flush on the underside of forewing.

LIFE STAGES: Females lay yellow, keg shaped, eggs on host plant leaves in late summer. Caterpillars hatch then hibernate until spring and begin feeding. Caterpillar is green-yellow with 4 yellow stripes on back and sides, a green head with short red forks in rear segment. Adult males patrol with a dipping flight. Adults sip flower nectar, wild geranium, thistle, and yellow composites, also rotting fruit and sap. The host plant is grasses. Flight May - September.

HABITAT: Moist grasslands, forest edges, open meadows, sagebrush flats, and slow watercoarses and marshes with long grasses.

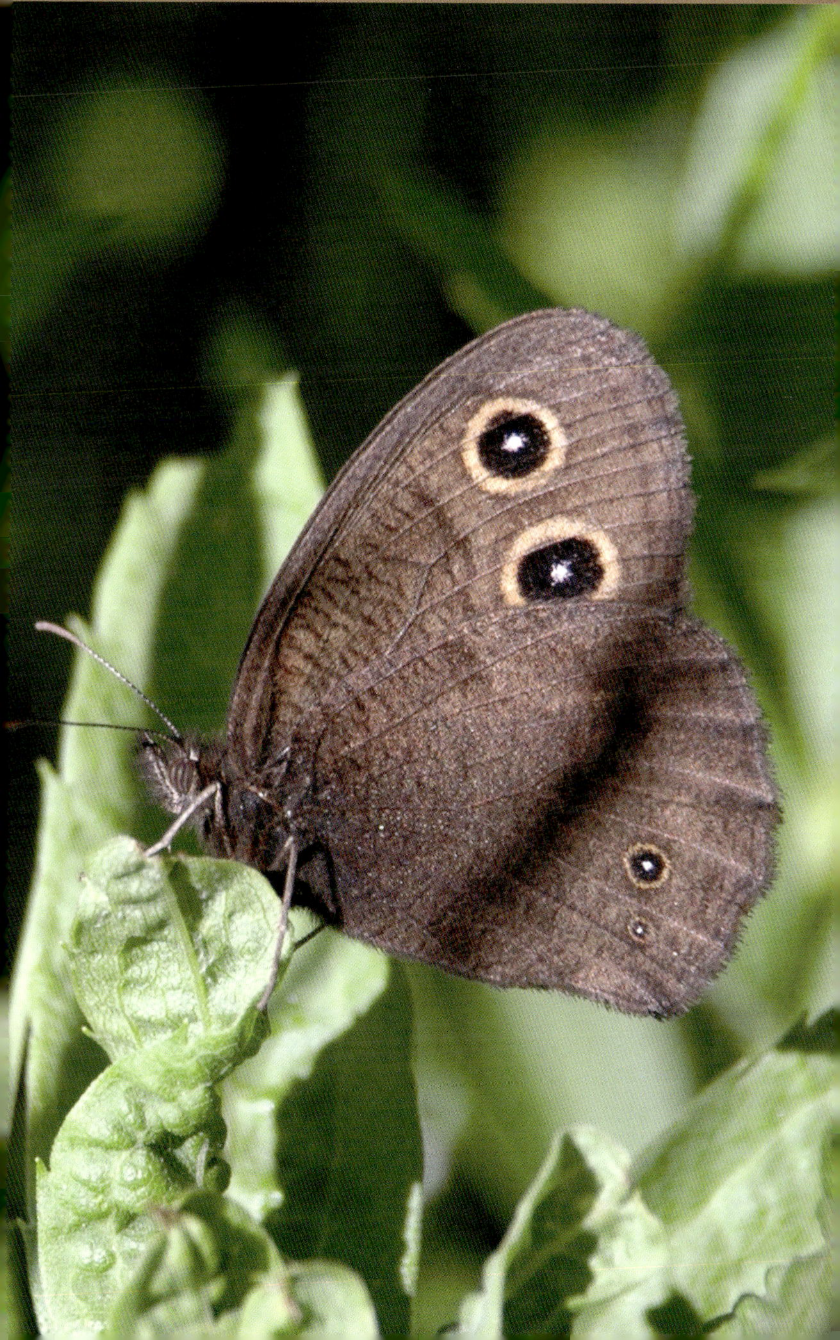

Common Alpine

Erebia epipsodea

IDENTIFICATION: Wing span 1½ - 2 inches. The most widespread Alpine. This species is the only one with eyespots on both wings. Upperside; dark brown, submarginal black eyespots with white centers surrounded by yellow-orange. Underside of forewing similar to upperside, hindwing usually frosted gray with eyespots. The similar Colorado Alpine lacks eyespots on hindwing.

LIFE STAGES: Eggs, yellow-white and spherical, laid in grasses. Caterpillar yellow-brown with stripes of yellow, or green with darker green stripes. Caterpillars probably eat grasses and late brood will hibernate. Flight from June thru August.

HABITAT: Open meadows and forests, sage flats, and moist areas.

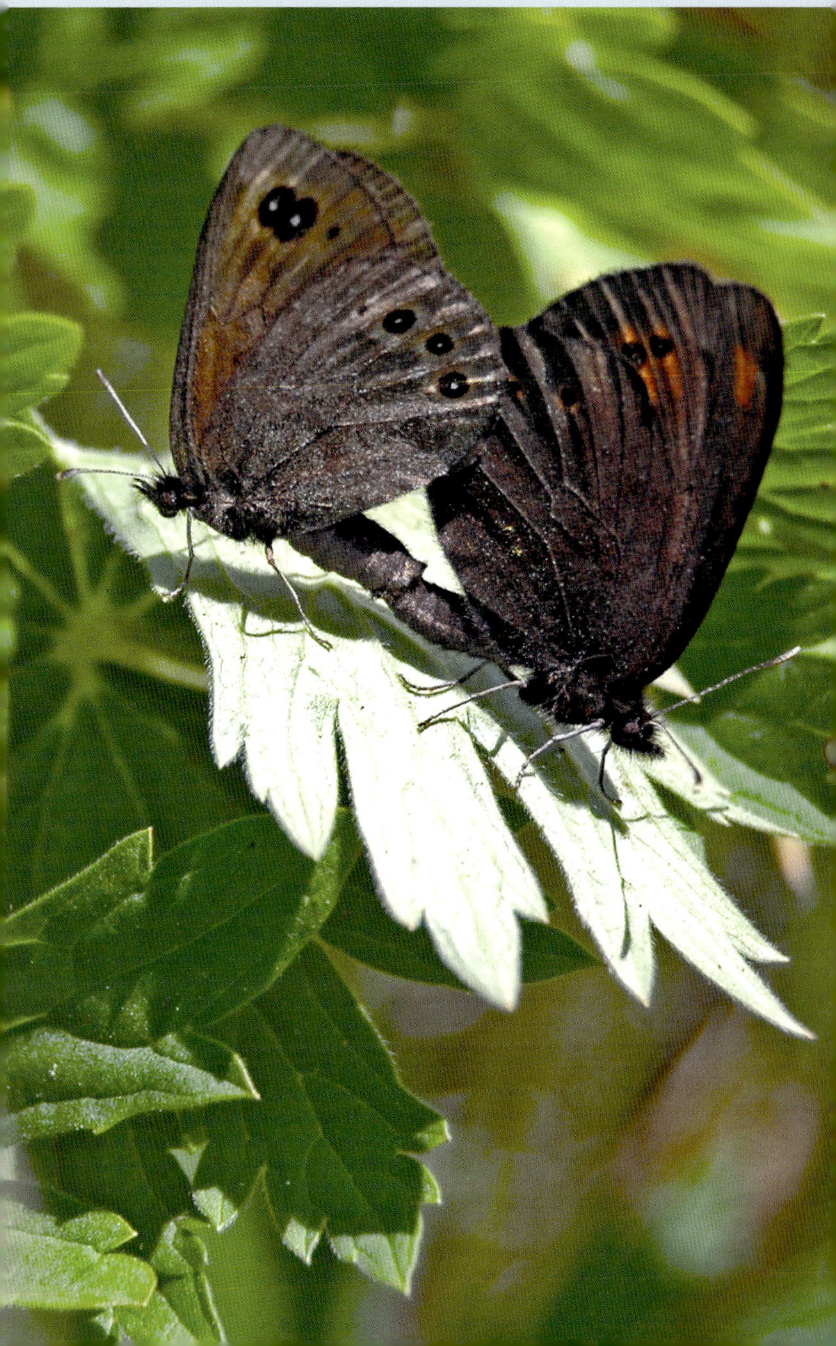

Magdalena Alpine

Erebia magdalena

IDENTIFICATION: Wing span 1¾ - 2 inches. Both wings without markings and black or dark brown in color. When recently hatched wings may have greenish iridescence. No similar species in our area.

LIFE STAGES: Not well reported. Yellow-brown egg laid on rocks or grasses. Caterpillar is green with short hairs and hibernates, but may take two years to mature. Probably feeds on grasses. Males patrol low above rockslides. Adult nectar at alpine flowers. Flight varies with snowmelt, late June to Early August.

HABITAT: Rockslide areas at or above timberline.

REMARKS: This is the only all dark, unmarked, butterfly that will be seen in its habitat.

Colorado Alpine

Erebia callias

IDENTIFICATION: Wing span
1⅜ - 1⅝ inches. Upperside; dark
brown with green iridescence, two
eyespots in orange patch on
forewing, submarginal orange and
black spots on hindwing. Underside; forewing similar to
upper but lighter, hindwing gray with black wavy lines.
Common Alpine similar but has more forewing eye spots.

LIFE STAGES: Single egg laid in grasses. Caterpillar brown
with darker lines and bands. Host probably grasses or sedges.
May mature over two years. Not well documented. Flight
July - August.

HABITAT: High elevation ridgelines and summit knobs with
grassy meadows.

Theano Alpine

Erebia theano

IDENTIFICATION: Wing span 1¼ - 1½ inches. Also named Yellow dotted Alpine (*Erebia pawloskii*). Small. Upperside; dark brown with post median band of red-orange spots on both wings, small cell spot. Underside similar to upper but spots lighter yellow-orange. No similar species all others have eyespots.

LIFE STAGES: Single egg laid in grass sedges or willows. Caterpillar tan with dark brown stripes and covered by thick hairs. Life stages not well documented. Adults perch in grasses and have low slow flight. Two years to mature in some populations, Wyoming colonies appear to mature in one year, will overwinter as larve. Flight July - August.

HABITAT: Alpine wetlands, bogs, and grassy openings in forest. Reported colonies on Togwotee pass east of Grand Teton Park and around Yellowstone lake in YNP.

Riding's Satyr

Neominois ridingsii

IDENTIFICATION: Wing span 1½ - 2 inches. Upperside; gray to gray brown with white ovals on outer wing between veins, one to three eye spots in forewing, may have hindwing eyespot. Underside; lighter tone, forewing similar, hindwing with striations and chevrons. No similar species.

LIFE STAGES: White keg shaped egg laid in grasses. Caterpillar red-tan with hairs and green banding, pupates in soil. Host probably grasses. Flight mid June - August. Adults fly low and quick, hiding in grass with folded wings.

HABITAT: Open sunny grasslands and sage flats.

Chryxus Arctic

Oeneis chryxus

IDENTIFICATION: Wing span 1½ - 2 inches. Upperside cream to orange brown with 1 - 4 eyespots near outer margin of forewing and 1 - 2 near anal angle of hindwing, these repeat on underside. Underside, forewing orange brown, hindwing with brown and gray striations and wider black marginal band. Veins are scaled white or gray. Similar to Uhler's Arctic which has more eyespots on hindwing.

LIFE STAGES: Host plants, poverty oat grass, sedges. Caterpillar requires two years to develop, is tan with red hairs and brown lateral stripes separated by white. Adults nectar at yellow flowers. This butterfly is well camouflaged and very wary, flying when approached. Flight June - August.

HABITAT: Forest openings, granite and limestone alpine slopes, and grassy meadows, usually near water.

White-veined Arctic

Oeneis bore

IDENTIFICATION: Wing span 1⅜ - 1⅞ inches. Also called *Oeneis taygete*. Translucent wings. Light gray brown upperside without marking. Underside; forewing apex lighter with diffuse marking at the end of the cell. Hindwing with broad median band outlined with black lines, white band on inner and outer sides, darker basal area and at margin, veins white. Similar to Melissa, Polixenes Arctics, which lack hindwing median band, Chryxus Arctic which has eyespots.

LIFE STAGES: Not well reported. Eggs laid on host probably grasses or sedges. Caterpillar light brown with dark brown, reddish and white lateral lines. Flight June - August.

HABITAT: Moist alpine meadows, grassy high ridges and summits.

Polixenes Arctic

Oeneis polixenes

IDENTIFICATION: Wing span 1½ - 2 inches. Wings translucent. Upperside, yellow to orange-brown, occasional row of small eyespots. Underside, gray brown, with median band darker and lined with white. Similar to Melissa Arctic and White-veined Arctic.

LIFE STAGES: Caterpillar brown with gray-green dorsal stripe and tan, black, and gray lateral stripes, head darker with stripes. Host plants sedges and grasses. Flight June thru August, may be biennial.

HABITAT: Open alpine or rocky tundra, grassy slopes with moist areas.

Jutta Arctic

Oeneis jutta

IDENTIFICATION: Wing span 1⅞ - 2⅛ inches. Upperside; gray brown with orange spots in submarginal band some with black eyespots. Diffuse dark sex patch on male forewing. Underside, forewing similar, hindwing mottled and striated with brown or darker gray, irregular median line.

LIFE STAGES: Yellowish egg laid in grass. Host probably sedges, cottongrass (*Eriophorum*). Caterpillar green with cream and olive stripes, red hairs and brown dots. Flight June - July.

HABITAT: Open glades in lodgepole forests, wet meadows with host sedge.

Melissa Arctic

Oeneis melissa

IDENTIFICATION: Wing span 1½ - 2 inches. Translucent wings are dull brown to gray on upperside. Wing fringes are checkered. Underside; forewing similar to upperside, hindwing is mottled or striated black and white, may have slightly darker median band. Usually no eyespots. Similar to Polixenes Arctic which is smaller with a darker hindwing medial band. White-veined Arctic is yellower and has the lightened veins on underside.

LIFE STAGES: Pale green-gray egg. Host Plant sedges (Carex). Caterpillar green with blue green and yellow green stripes on back and down sides. Head is brown. Both egg and larve reported to hibernate. May be biennial. Flight late June - August depending on conditions. Not active fliers.

HABITAT: Found above 10,000 ft in alpine meadows, windswept ridges, rockslides, and summits.

Persius Duskywing

Erynnis persius

IDENTIFICATION: Wing span 1 - 1¼ inches. Brown-black. Markings on male more obscured than on female. Upperside; forewing with gray patch and four white dots at end of cell, white hairs on wing with a pattern of dots. Hindwing with brown fringe, submarginal spots brown or buff. Very similar to Afranius Duskywing which lacks white hairs and has pale tips on fringes.

LIFE STAGES: Green egg changes to pink before hatching. Caterpillar light green with white specks, and red-yellow head. Host plants lupine, vetches or other legumes. Adult males perch on ridges to await females. Flight April - July or early August.

HABITAT: Forest openings, meadows, roadcuts, and streamsides.

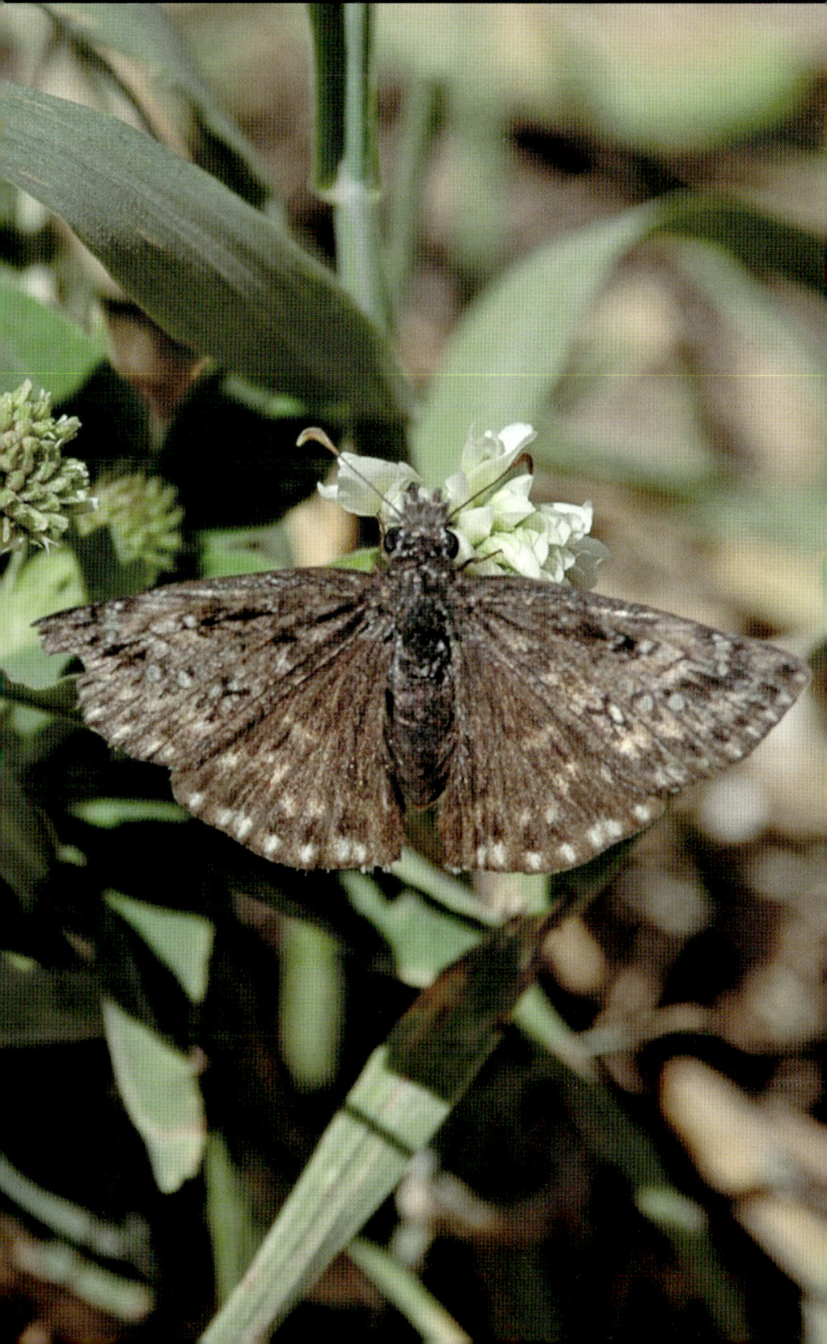

Afranius Duskywing

Erynnis afranius

IDENTIFICATION: Wing span ⅞ - 1½ inches. Upperside brownish-black, forewing with pale overscaling and some clear spots. Hindwing fringe is pale tipped. Similar to Persius Duskywing which has long white scaling on forewing and will perch on hilltops.

LIFE STAGES: Eggs laid on underside of host plant leaves. Caterpillar is pale green to yellow-green with white dots, a yellow line on sides and a dark line on back. Males perch in gullies or swales. Host plants legumes such as lupine and milkvetch. Flight April thru August. Adults sip flower nectar, frequent muddy areas.

HABITAT: Opening and edges in forest, steamcourses, moist areas.

Dreamy Duskywing

Erynnis icelus

IDENTIFICATION: Wing span 1 – 1⅜ inches. Dark brown to black. Two differences from other duskywings are the labial palpi are long and point forward and no transparent spots in forewing. Upperside, forewing has gray scales with post median bands of black spots, hindwing has two rows of pale spots. Underside is similar. Persius and Afranius Duskywings are similar. Noted differences above.

LIFE STAGES: Green ribbed egg laid singly on host. Caterpillar green with short white hair in clumps, head with red and yellow markings. Caterpillar will make leaf shelters and overwinters. Host plants willow (*Salix*) and Aspen (*Populus*). Adults like mud puddles and flower nectar. Flight April – July.

HABITAT: Forest roadsides, trails, and clearings, also along watercourses.

European Skipper

Thymelicus lineola

IDENTIFICATION: Wing span 1 - 1⅛ inches. Upperside, brown-orange with black borders and outer portion of veins lined black. Fringes orange-brown and underside of head and thorax whiter. Underside, wings lighter orange-tan with no markings. Similar species, Garita Skipperling has light marking on veins of underside hindwing.

LIFE STAGES: Up to 30 eggs laid in row on stalk or seedhead of host grass. Eggs hibernate. Caterpillar green, with a dark dorsal stripe and yellow vertical stripes on front. Head is brown. Host plant grasses, primarily Timothy grass. Adults nectar at flowers. Flight May - July.

HABITAT: Open meadows, fields, and pastures with Timothy grass, roadsides, forest clearings and trails.

Two-Banded Checkered Skipper

Pyrgus ruralis

IDENTIFICATION: Wing span $\frac{3}{4}$ - 1 inch. Checkered fringes. Upperside, brown black with small white spots that form a broken X on forewing, hindwing spots in median and submarginal rows with a very small white spot near base on hindwing. Underside, brownish gray with forewing spots similar to upperside and hindwing spots but more mottled. Similar to Grizzled Skipper which is larger.

LIFE STAGES: Eggs laid singly on host plant, horkelias or cinquefoils. Caterpillars form leaf nests. Adults sip flower nectar. Males patrol for females and perch low to ground. Flight May thru July.

HABITAT: Open meadows and dry forest clearings in higher elevations.

Common Checkered Skipper

Pyrgus communis

IDENTIFICATION: Wing span ⅞ - 1¼ inches. Fringes checkered black at vein ends, but black may only reach halfway in fringe. Upperside of most males with blue-gray tone, females black with smaller white spots. Both sexes with white spots in median band across both wings. Both wings have spots in marginal rows that are smaller than spots in submarginal row. Underside dull white with rows of black outlined gray or brown bands of variable width.

LIFE STAGES: Females lay a single egg on leaves of host. Caterpillar with black hairy head and white to brown body, lateral lines, and covered with small white bumps. Caterpillars make folded leaf nests, hibernate. Host plants in mallow family including hollyhock. Adults sip nectar. Flight April - September.

HABITAT: Open sunny places with low vegetation such as, yards, meadows, roadcuts, trails, preference for areas with bare ground.

COMMON CHECKERED SKIPPER

Northern White Skipper

Heliopetes ericetorum

IDENTIFICATION: Wing span 1 - 1½ inches. Fringes tan-white with dark at vein endings. Veins may have brown-black scaling. Upperside, white with black-brown chevrons in margin, female with darker markings and black at wing base. Underside, white with broad irregular brown bands and brown base, chevrons at anal angle of hindwing. No similar species in our area.

LIFE STAGES: Single egg laid on host plant. Caterpillar has black head and light green-yellow body with faint stripe on back and side. Caterpillar lives in rolled leaf shelter. Host plant, hollyhock or other mallows. Adults perch low to ground and nectar at flowers. Flight May - September.

HABITAT: Arid land, mountain forest openings, roadcuts, meadows.

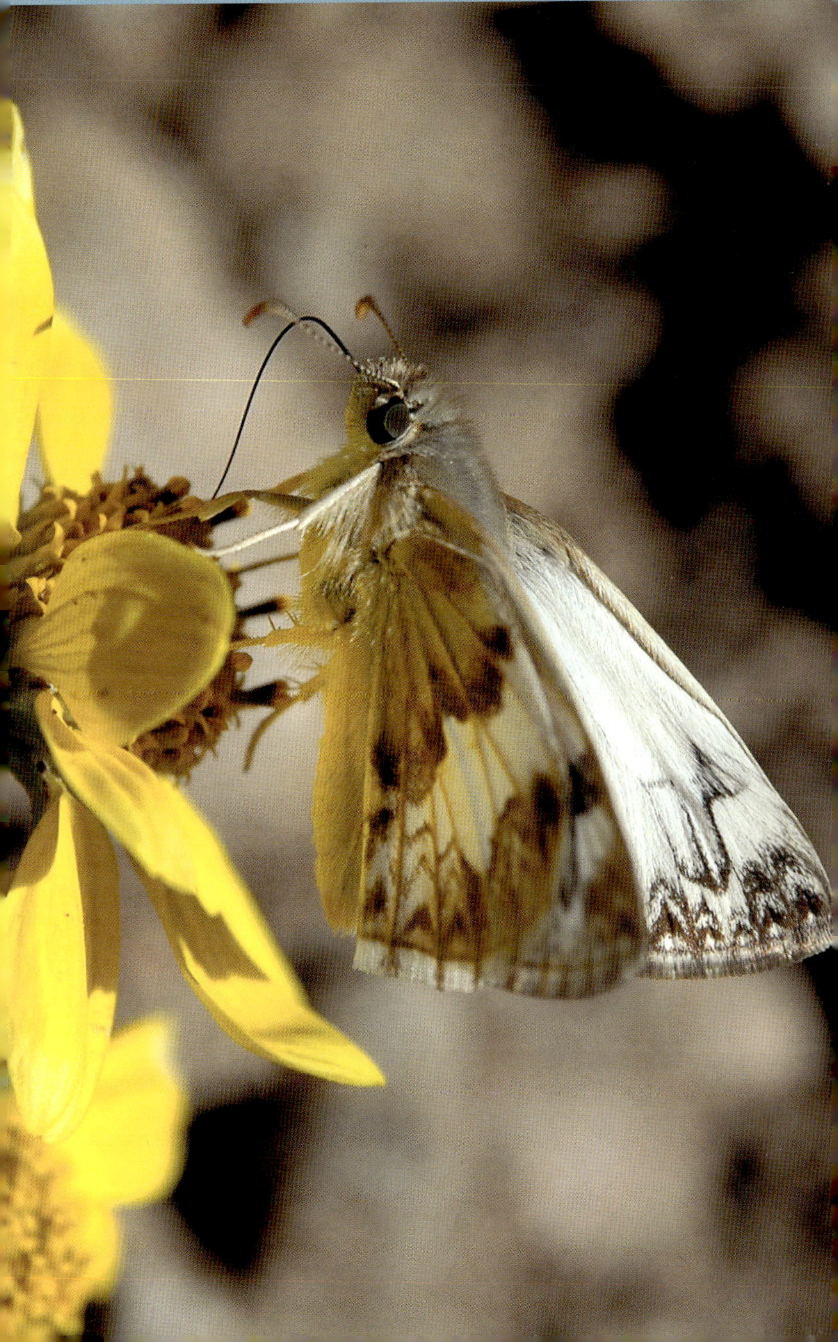

Common Sootywing

Pholisora catullus

IDENTIFICATION: Wing span 1 - 1½ inches. Upperside, black with small white spots on outer third of forewing; female with more spots and row on hindwing. Underside repeats pattern of upperside. No similar species in our area.

LIFE STAGES: Single egg laid on top of host leaves. Caterpillar green with raised pale dots and black head. Host plants, in family amaranthaceae and chenopodiaceae. Second brood of caterpillar hibernates in leaf nest. Adults bask with wings open and nectar at flowers. Flight May - August.

HABITAT: Open spaces, disturbed areas, fields roadsides, gardens.

COMMON SOOTYWING

Arctic Skipper

Carterocephalus palaemon

IDENTIFICATION: Wing span 1 - 1¼ inches. Upperside is black, checkered with squared orange spots. Underside forewing orange with black spots, hindwing orange-brown with black outlined white spots.

LIFE STAGES: Single egg laid on host plant leaf. Caterpillar white or green with darker green line on back and yellow lines enclosed by dark spots on sides. Caterpillars make silk nest in leaves and will overwinter in nest. Host plant grasses. Adults sip nectar and will hold wings open while basking. Flight May - July.

HABITAT: Edges and openings in forest, streamside, and moist areas.

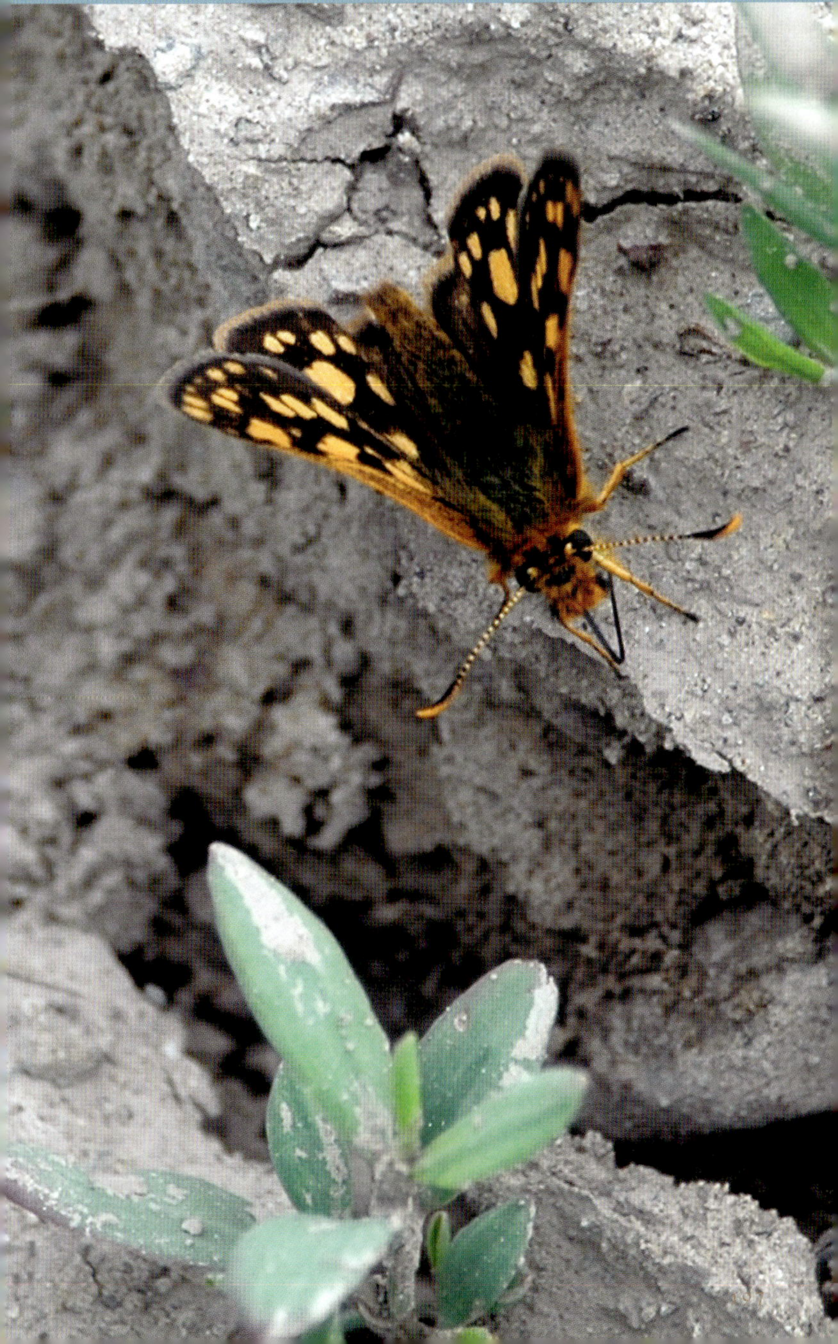

Juba Skipper

Hesperia juba

IDENTIFICATION: Wing span 1¼ - 1⅝ inches. Upperside, orange-brown, a dark marginal pattern with sharp margins extends inward in toothed pattern between veins. Male stigma has interior white felt. Underside, hindwing green-brown with larger white spots that extend slightly along veins, lowest submarginal spot in band is offset inwardly. Forewing with more orange-brown, two white spots matching upperside position. Similar to Western Branded and Nevada skippers, neither has as sharp a upperside border pattern or offset hindwing spot.

LIFE STAGES: Single egg on or near host, Caterpillar cream-tan with dark head and stripes on face. Caterpillar makes leaf shelter, may hibernate. Host plant grasses. Flight May - September, two broods.

HABITAT: Sagebrush flats or grassy openings in pine forest.

Male stigma on forewing

Nevada Skipper

Hesperia nevada

IDENTIFICATION: Wing span 1 - 1⅜ inches. Upperside; tawny orange to brown orange with darker border gradually blending into base color. Male with black sigma. Underside hindwing green to gray with irregular crescent shaped white spots, spot near base offset inward more than similar species. Juba Skipper larger with more pointed forewing.

LIFE STAGES: White egg laid near host, bunch grasses. Caterpillar green to brown with black head having white markings. Flight in June - July.

HABITAT: Higher elevations 7000 - 12,000 ft. sagebrush, alpine meadows, forest edges.

Western Branded Skipper

Hesperia colorado

IDENTIFICATION: Wing span ⅞ - 1⅜ inches. The most variable of the 15 western Hesperia species. Only the Nevada Skipper is similar in our area. Forewing often pointed. Upperside broad dark border and orange background. Males forewing stigma with black scaling. Underside color variable from greenish, orange-red, brown or gray with white chevron and spots of variable size.

LIFE STAGES: Eggs scattered singly near host plant. Caterpillar tan with brown head. Caterpillar eats leaves and has silken nest at base of host. Host plants sedges and several grasses. Adults sip nectar at flowers. Flight July - September.

HABITAT: Grasslands, forest openings and edges, alpine tundra, sage meadows and fields.

Draco Skipper

Polites draco

IDENTIFICATION: Wing span $\frac{7}{8}$ – $1\frac{1}{4}$ inches. Upperside; Male has broad dark brown band on outer wing, red orange on leading edge and base with S shaped black sigma bordered with gray scales. Female darker coloring. Underside; orange to greenish coloring with a few spots on forewing and a large chevron shaped series of linked paler spots on hindwing. No similar species in this area.

LIFE STAGES: Not much information. Caterpillar reported as dark brown with black bands and a black head. Host plant grasses. Adults nectar at flowers. Flight June – August.

HABITAT: Higher elevation, alpine and sub alpine dry grassy meadows, streamside mud puddles.

Sonora Skipper

Polites sonora

IDENTIFICATION: Wing span ¾ - 1¼ inches. Upperside; brown and orange with broad diffuse dark border, male with black stigma an broad black adjacent patch. Underside; varies from olive thru tan to red-brown, distinctive feature is crescent shaped medial row of lighter spots with one or two basal spots. Draco Skipper has S shaped stigma and elongated spots in hindwing center. Long Dash has elongated spots on hindwing underside.

LIFE STAGES: Caterpillar green with black head. Host plant grasses, Idaho fescue. Adults males perch in low areas. Flight June - September.

HABITAT: Open moist meadows, watercourses and roadcuts in forest openings.

Woodland Skipper

Ochlodes sylvanoides

IDENTIFICATION: Wing span 1 - 1¼ inches. Upperside; tawny orange and black, prominent black stigme (male) and dash (female) and dark margin with inward toothed border extending between veins. Underside; variable, reddish brown to yellow-orange, submarginal band of cream colored squarish spots not always visible in lighter wing tones. Similar to Long Dash which flies earlier.

LIFE STAGES: Ivory color egg laid in host grasses. Caterpillar light green with dark dorsal and yellow lateral lines or yellow with dark bands, head is cream color with black stripe. Chrysalid cocoa and gray. Host wheat grass, bermuda grass, and wildrye among others. Flight July - October.

HABITAT: Many open areas with grasses, sagebrush, small watercourses, and woodlands.

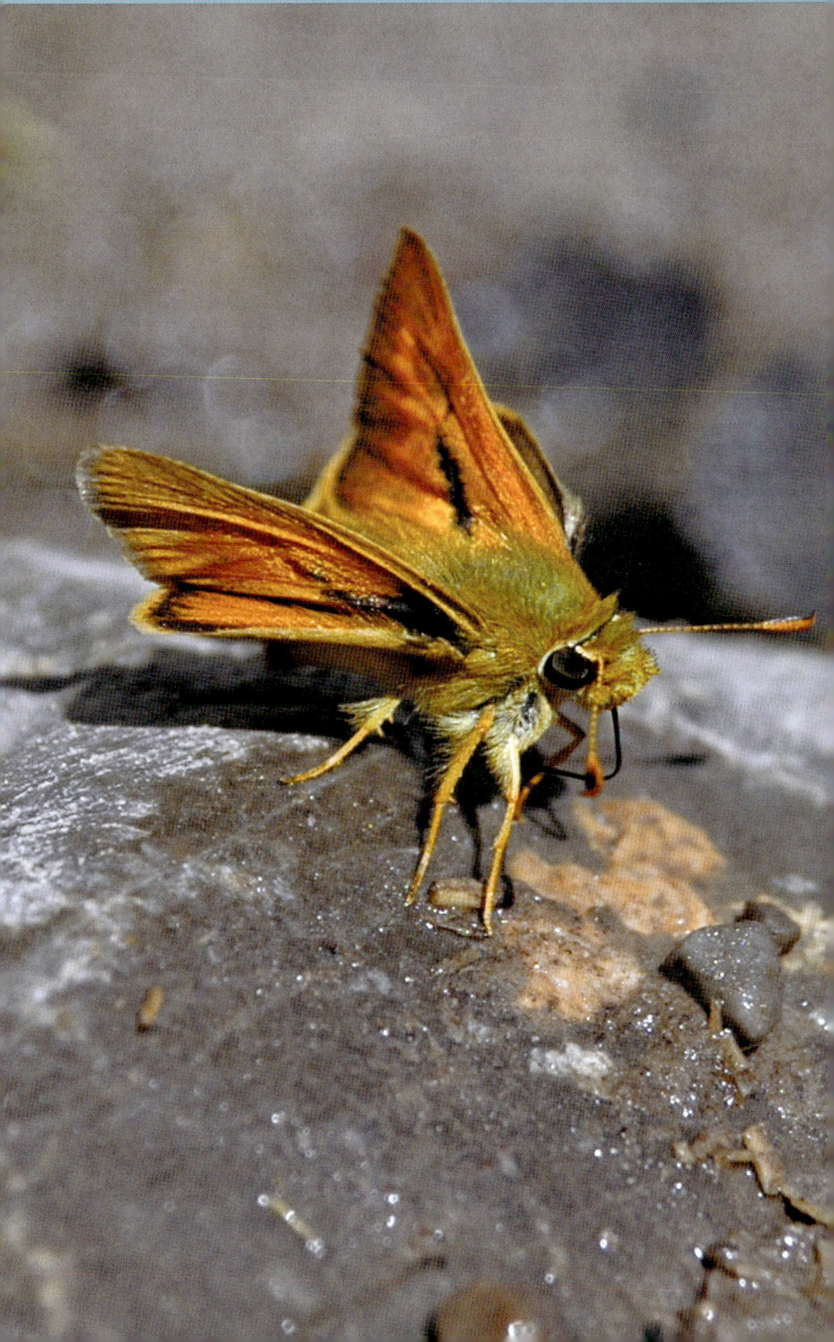

Pecks Skipper

Polites peckius

IDENTIFICATION: Wing span ¾ - 1¼ inches. Also called the Yellowpatch Skipper (*Polites coras*) in some guides. Upperside dark brown with wide orange costal margin, hindwing has central orange patch, male has curved black sigma. Underside, hindwing lighter brown orange with wide, well defined, yellow-tan bands above the base and post median, divided with a broken median bar of base color. No species with similar markings.

LIFE STAGES: Single green egg. Caterpillar maroon with brown markings, head black with white markings. Makes leaf shelter. Host plant grasses. Adult nectars at flowers and sips from moist ground. Flight June - August.

HABITAT: Open grassy areas, meadows, roadsides, marshes.

Tawny-Edged Skipper

Polites themistocles

IDENTIFICATION: Wing span ⅞ – 1½ inches. Dark brown with tawny orange on costal edge of forewing. Male sigma double curved. Female may be darker. Underside hindwing, plain, mustard to green to gray. May be confused with Draco Skipper on upperside, but underside very different.

LIFE STAGES: Single egg on host grass. Caterpillar maroon to brown with two vertical lines on head. Pupae overwinters. Host grasses, bluegrass, crabgrass, panic grass. Flight June – July.

HABITAT: Moist mountain grasslands, lawns, pastures, and roadsides.

References

PRINT:

Butterflies of the Rocky Mountain States, C. Ferris and F. Brown, U of OK Press, 1981

A Field Guide to Western Butterflies (Peterson), P. Opler and A. Wright, Houghton Mifflin, 1999

A Field Guide to Butterflies of the Greater Yellowstone Ecosystem, by Diane Debinski, James A. Pritchard, and Lynn Thorensen, Roberts Rinehart, 2002

National Audubon Society Field Guide to North American Butterflies, R. Pyle consulting, Chanticleer Press. 1981

Butterflies of the World, G. Martin and M. Baran, Abrams, 2006

American Butterflies (Quarterly publication), North American Butterfly Association (NABA), editor J. Glassberg. Multiple volumes, various years

An Obsession with Butterflies. S Russell, Perseus Publishing, 2003

Nabokov's Butterflies, R. Pyle, Beacon Press, 2000

Plants of Yellowstone and Grand Teton National Parks, R. Shaw, Wheelwright Press, 1981

A Field Guide to Rocky Mountain Wildflowers (Peterson), J. Craighead, F. Craighead, R. Davis, Houghton Mifflin, 1963

Stokes Butterfly Book, Donald and Lillian Stokes, Ernest Williams, Little Brown and Company, 2007

INTERNET:

Opler, Paul A., Harry Pavulaan, Ray E. Stanford< Michael Pogue, coordinators. 2006. Butterflies and Moths of North America. Bozeman, MT: NBII Mountain Prairie Information Node, *http://www.butterfliesandmoths.org*

The Xerces Society, *www.xerces.org*

University of Alberta, entomology collection, *www.entomology.ualberta.ca*

Government of Canada, Canadian Biodiversity Information Facility, Butterflies of Canada, *www.cbif.gc.ca*

Nearctica.com the natural history of North America, *www.nearctica.com*

Colorado butterflies photo gallery by Tom Murray at pbase.com, *www.pbase.com*

UK Natural History Museum, Cockayne Collection, *www.nhm.ac.uk/index.html*

The Butterfly Website, *www.butterflywebsite.com*

Warren, A. D., K.J. Davis, J.P. Pelham, E.M. Strangeland. 2008. Interactive listing of American Butterflies, 10-30-2008. *www.butterfliesofamerica.com*

enature.com, *www.enature.com*

Art Shapiro's Butterfly site, *www.butterfly.ucdavis.edu/*

Wisconsin Butterflies, *www.wisconsinbutterflies.org*

North American Butterfly Association, *www.naba.org*

USGS, Northern Prairie Wildlife Research Center, *www.npwrc.usgs.gov/*

ABOUT THE AUTHOR

Steve Poole lives in Wilson, Wyoming with his wife and daughter. He loves to be out in the wild biking, hiking, boating, skiing, and watching the natural world while trying to capture some magnificent part on his camera.

Steve Poole

Emily Poole

Please don't collect butterflies. *Not only are they protected within Grand Teton and Yellowstone National Parks so the next person can enjoy them, but they provide pollination and their eggs create new butterflies for next season.*

All natural features of the park are protected. Rocks, driftwood, and animal bones or antlers are part of the land and should be left where found.

Staying on the trails not only protects the vegetation and helps prevent erosion, but it also gives wildlife a sense of where to expect humans.
